INNER CHILD HEALING

DISCOVER YOUR TRUE SELF, OVERCOME
CHILDHOOD TRAUMA, AND DEEPEN
RELATIONSHIPS WITH SELF-LOVE, CHAKRA
HEALING, AND TWIN FLAME CONNECTION

S. M. WENG

CONTENTS

Introduction   vii
BONUS MATERIAL   xiii

1. WHO IS YOUR INNER CHILD?   1
   The Birth of Your Inner Child   1
   Modern Ideas About the Inner Child   5
   Inner Child Development   6

2. DISCERNMENT—IDENTIFYING THE SOURCE
   OF YOUR WOUNDS   15
   Habitual Loops or Triggers   16
   What Is the Self?   19
   How Do Your Beliefs About Yourself, Others,
   and the World Around You Affect How You Feel
   and Think?   26
   The Body's Stress Response   27
   How Do You Create a Better Self-Concept?   34

3. CALLING OUT THE INNER CHILD AND
   LISTENING TO WHAT IT SCREAMS   36
   What Is Your Inner Child's Voice?   36
   Taking Your Inner Voice Seriously   40
   Questionnaire: Is Your Inner Child Wounded?   47

4. HOW YOUR INNER CHILD CRIES OUT   51
   How Do Your Inner Child's Wounds Affect Your
   Happiness?   52
   How Do Your Inner Child's Wounds Affect Your
   Finances?   53
   How Does a Wounded Inner Child Affect
   Relationships?   54
   How Does a Wounded Inner Child Affect Your
   Career?   57
   How Do the Inner Child's Wounds Influence
   Your Parenting?   58

   A Moment of Reflection   61

5. UNLOCK YOUR INNER CHILD'S HEALING
POWER—TRANSFORM YOUR HABITS AND
REINFORCE BOUNDARIES TO ACHIEVE
LASTING CHANGE! 63
 H—Harvest Your Inner Child's Needs 63
 E—Explore the Twin Flame Journey 72
 A—Activate Your Boundaries 77
 L—Lead Your New Habits Consciously 81

6. EXPLORE THE TWIN FLAME JOURNEY FOR
INNER CHILD HEALING 86
 Use Reparenting to Unite Your Twin Flame
 Connection 87

7. ACTIVATE YOUR BOUNDARIES TO PROTECT
THE PRECIOUS INNER CHILD 91
 What Benefits Come From Setting Realistic
 Goals and Boundaries? 92
 How Do You Begin Choosing New Goals and
 Boundaries? 93
 Setting Your Boundaries for Nine Types of Inner
 Child Healing 95
 Build and Reserve Your Boundaries in Small
 Steps 106
 Be Wise, Don't Catastrophize 107

8. LEAD YOUR NEW HABITS TO HEAL THE
INNER CHILD'S WOUNDS 110
 How to Use the Seven Chakras to Heal Your
 Inner Child 110

Your Chance to Help Another Inner Child 125
Conclusion 127
Author Bio 129
References 131
Also by S. M. Weng 135

INTRODUCTION

The only path by which another person can upset you is through your own thought. –Joseph Murphy

Your subconscious mind, also known as your inner child, is responsible for controlling about 95% of your life (Positive Creators, 2020). This means that if you are only consciously managing 5% of your thoughts, you may not feel like you have much control. Because of this, you might feel insecure, under-appreciated, ashamed, or guilty for no apparent reason.

It sounds like you're going through a lot right now. After all, that's why you purchased this book—to assist you. You may feel like you're constantly walking on eggshells, trying to please others, and avoid conflict. It can be difficult to let go of things and embrace new experiences when you're struggling with anxiety and self-doubt. Perhaps you feel like you're always striving for perfection but can never quite get there. When you're feeling overwhelmed and unsure of your worth, it's normal to worry about your ability to keep healthy relation-ships or handle your money. It's clear that you're carrying a heavy burden, and you're deeply afraid of being rejected or abandoned. Please know that your feelings are valid, and it's acceptable to seek support whenever you require.

My name is Susye; I saw these kinds of issues being mentioned among my social media followers, and I could relate, as I have faced many similar challenges in my own life. When I was merely four years old, my parents got angry with me and told me that I was behaving badly, although I would deem my behavior to have been normal in relation to what most kids of that age do. What really hurt me the most is that they told me that they would throw me away. It made me feel worthless and scared.

One day, while we were driving in the car, far away from home on an unfamiliar road, they stopped the car, opened the door, and told me to get out. They left me abandoned on the side of a bridge in Brazil and drove away. My parents drove around the block for a good five to ten minutes, which felt like hours to me, before coming back to pick me up. However, as a four year old, this caused me great stress and fear. This became one of my triggers in life, as I feared being abandoned again, causing me to experience separation anxiety throughout my life whenever someone I deemed to be my security left me unattended for a short while. This would activate my fear and cause great insecurities to arise.

As a four-year-old girl, I panicked, and unknowingly, I never recovered from this event. It was only much later in life, as an adult, when I got into inner child meditation to unblock my fear of abandonment, where I made peace with that experience.

Because I experienced much of the same things as many of my followers, I was determined to find answers as to why I felt something deep inside me was wrong. I had to know why I responded and behaved the way I did and why I believed certain things when others questioned my beliefs. I saw too much turmoil among my followers and in my own life. I then decided to travel and use my experiences as opportunities to find answers in ancient practices.

I was married for 28 years, but due to my unhealed inner child wounds, I had many fears and ended up self-sabotaging my marriage. After my divorce, I went on a spiritual journey and connected with my twin flame. It wasn't until I healed my inner child that I understood all that was holding me back from reaching my full potential in life. My followers and my own past inspired me to write about healing my inner child, and on my travels, I learned about many holistic, mindful, and spiritual techniques.

I tried and tested many methods, took advice from psychology and spiritualism, and spent time perfecting my approach. I used Western and Eastern culture to design a unique "HEAL" process with practical tips you can follow daily, and I uniquely focus on inner child meditation to complete the integration and healing process.

People like me and my followers aren't the only ones who've had trouble getting over past traumas. Drew Barrymore, a well-known Hollywood celebrity, also experienced struggles during her childhood. Recently, her fans were thrilled to see a carefree and happy video of her enjoying the rain while reflecting on her tough past. The video of the actress-turned-talk-show-host frolicking in the rain went viral on social media. In the video, she urged her fans to do the same if they ever get the chance. Her positive attitude and original point of view on life inspired many people. However, the video also sparked a conversation about Barrymore's difficult childhood and experiences as a child star in Hollywood. One fan even commented that "nobody is working harder to heal their inner child than Drew Barrymore."

By reading *Inner Child Healing*, you can achieve a life that is free from the burdens of your past wounds and struggles that your inner child carries. This will allow you to become the person you truly want to be, to believe in what you want, and to behave in ways that align with your true desires. With the information in the book, you can learn to control your inner child and build a good relationship with it, which will give you lasting peace of mind.

You'll discover the following:

- Why you are the way you are and who your inner child is.
- The psychology that sets your beliefs in stone.
- Why your inner child reacts as it does.
- How your life suffers because of a wounded inner child, who needs healing.
- The ways to identify your inner child's wounds.
- Recognizing the most common issues due to inner child traumas.
- Finding a healing path through the HEAL journey.
- The steps you'll need to reparent your inner child and heal its trauma.
- Discerning your journey to bring the twin flames back together.
- Setting boundaries that enforce new habits.
- Integration models that encourage chakra healing and meditation.

I'm taking a new route in life, challenging the twin flame journey, to bring karma and luck back to my inner child, where things once looked bleak. Chakra healing, a spiritual method, built on top of a psychological foundation, isn't a commonly known strategy, but I can pledge that it works.

Inner Child Healing will help you discover three simple steps to healing your inner child while discovering what caused it to become what it is, and you'll find lasting benefits from practicing the everyday, practical advice to love yourself, heal from the past, and shine your brightest light for everyone else.

Finding the path to your healed inner child will be narrow and challenging, but an understanding of what went wrong is definitely where you should start. Then, you can take action with three simple steps to heal your inner child's wounds. Does that sound like your deepest desire? If so, please join me on this journey through the foundation of what designs your inner child.

BONUS MATERIAL

Dear Readers,

Thank you for choosing my book *INNER CHILD HEALING*. As a special gift to you, I am including this BONUS MATERIAL, which you can access here:

https://www.smwengbooks.com

I hope that this book serves as a guiding light on your inner child's spiritual journey. Inner child healing isn't merely a buzzword; it's a profound and evidence-based approach rooted in psychology and therapy. It encourages us to delve into our past, understand and heal emotional wounds, ultimately transforming our future for a brighter tomorrow.

As a token of my gratitude for choosing my book, I'm delighted to provide you with this BONUS MATERIAL as a special gift. Please be sure to download this valuable resource!

Sending you love and light,
S. M. Weng

1

WHO IS YOUR INNER CHILD?

The first half of life is devoted to forming a healthy ego; the second half is going inward and letting go of it. –Carl Jung

You know that annoying little voice in your head that constantly bugs you? Your inner child never sleeps, even when you do. It's true; an inner child didn't just pop into your head overnight. Instead, it took years of conditioning, as shown in psychology and holistic practices. So, keeping a conscious eye on the inner child is impossible, and it's always learning, absorbing, and determining what to do next. So, let's discover who your inner child is, where they came from, and how conditioning turned them into the wounded soul you are encountering today.

The Birth of Your Inner Child

Who is this inner child? What does it mean to work with and cure our inner child? We talk about the historical past of the notion of the "inner child," its various interpretations, as well as the independence that results from learning to know oneself better.

Psychology and Philosophy: A Historical Perspective—The Inner Child Idea

Most people think that Carl Jung (1875–1961) was the first person to use the term "inner child" (Pikörn, 2019). Jung describes many archetypes, including the divine child. Jung disagreed with the notion that we enter this planet as blank checks. Instead, he thought that everyone has "primordial images" that were already there before we were born. This concept is mentioned in Eastern philosophies as well as the concept of previous and future lives. The collective unconscious is expressed through Jungian archetypes as well. They are potentials that manifest as behaviors and interactions with the outer environment when they enter consciousness. The archetype is a subconscious part of who we are that drives how we act.

In widely known cognitive science, the "inner child" persona is like an unconscious component of our personality that is made up of what we learned and went through when we were youngsters (Pikörn, 2019). This personality of the inner child is below the conscious mind, but it still influences it. If the inner child is badly upset, hurt, or worried, the effect will be bad.

Jungian psychotherapy's role is to repair this inner child. Through a process called "reparenting," psychotherapists can help their patients to get an understanding of the trauma and pain of their inner child. By working with this inner child in a compassionate manner and showing them unique ways to act, the adult is no longer compelled to act on the wants of the wild, subconscious child.

Fulfilling the Needs of the Inner Child

Roberto Assagioli, who came up with the term "psychosynthesis" in the early 1900s to describe the study of one's soul and personality, thought that it was important for the healthy growth of the ego to heal from childhood trauma, but that the goal of "self-realization" and spiritual experiences were also important for human growth (Pikörn, 2019).

Abraham Maslow's hierarchy of wants placed self-actualization at the top, which contributed to its popularity. According to Maslow's theory, people's potential can start to be realized once their basic needs—such as those for food, water, and shelter—have been met (Pikörn, 2019).

These psychotherapists from the past might well have affirmed that "self-actualization," or achieving our full potential, can't happen until we make peace with the kid inside of us and their needs.

Eastern Philosophies and Your Inner Child, Including the Concept of Karma and Rebirth

Karma and Your Inner Child

The laws of karma teach us that we are born again because we didn't complete our mission in a past life. Additionally, because needs we don't realize we have already met are what motivate our actions in the present, this cycle keeps repeating itself in our lives.

The scarred inner child longs to be healed. The kid within us who remains in anger, anguish, fear, guilt, rage, or humiliation either flees from the world or lashes out at it because they can't handle all of these strong feelings. It might be based on rigid thinking and strong beliefs as a way to keep them safe from the world. Kindness and adult guidance are needed for them to learn to trust and feel complete. Our problems from the past will keep coming back until we heal our inner child. Karma says that we will keep doing the same things until we decide to stop. Jung may have talked about the inner child's "hidden subconscious forces," but Eastern philosophers talk about how karma begins. Such seeds are safely planted in our subconscious, and they will keep growing and turn into bad things until we make a choice to substitute them with healthy seeds or free them through self-healing.

The rewarding news is that you, the parent, have set free the child in you. Yes, just like the seeds of karma, the latent abilities of the inner child archetype can also be restored. We can plant the seeds for good karma, and the good qualities of an inner child who has been healed can help us. A healed, healthy inner child can stay in the present, doesn't hold on to inside-the-box beliefs, and is okay with letting go. Our inner child is curious, likes to play, and sees the funny side of serious situations. By reconnecting, it may lead us to a more fulfilling life.

Your Inner Child Healed

The inner child wants help. This is the basis of Buddhist psychology. We cannot reach our destiny in life if we don't heal our inner child first. The Buddhist spiritual leader says that we should use mindfulness to listen to our inner child with kindness (Hanh, 2010).

In Buddhist philosophy, consciousness is split into two categories: active (mental) awareness, and our root awareness, which is similar to the subconsciousness, where our seeds of karma are kept and where our inner child lives. We have the chance to make our minds more aware every day.

Every day, we have the chance to build up our mind's awareness by meditating and doing even the most boring tasks with full attention. As our awareness grows, we will hear our inner child's voice more clearly. The first steps toward reconciliation are to pay attention and listen. As soon as we admit that we have an inner child crying out for help, we can take care of them and reparent them with self-love and compassion.

Modern Ideas About the Inner Child

These days there are many therapists and a multitude of online resources available to assist with inner child healing. How fortunate are we?

The term "inner child" doesn't imply that you have a small child residing inside you or that a part of your brain thinks like a child. The core principle is that all of us have a part of our unconscious mind that is like a child. One way to think of the inner child is as our "subpersonality" (Jacobson, 2017). This is a part of your personality that can come out when you're in trouble.

The "ugly" and "pleasant" parts of the child we once were show up in our inner child. We still have feelings and needs from when we were kids that haven't been met. We also still have the innocence, creativity, and joy we had as kids. If you wanted to be liked as a child, you were told not to feel specific emotions. So, if you only got attention when you were "good," your inner child might be full of anger, heartbreak, and rebellion. Perhaps, if you had been mistreated or abused, you might have learned to hide your pain and fear in a bid to remain alive. The inner child can also hide all the things our parents, teachers, or other adults told us to think about ourselves. This can sound like "you're not good enough" or "don't do that, it's too difficult." Getting in touch with your inner child can help you figure out where your problems as a grownup come from. Working on your inner child can help you find and let go of repressed emotions that are holding you back, figure out what your unmet needs are, break bad habits, be more creative and playful, and have more self-respect.

There are many ways to heal emotional and psychological problems these days. Some types of therapy don't talk about the past or the idea of an "inner child." Cognitive behavioral therapy is one example. It focuses more on how your actions, feelings, and thoughts are connected.

Inner Child Development

Where does your inner child start, and how does it learn to behave the way it does? Since birth, before you could even make conscious decisions, your inner child has been getting messages. Often these messages are harmful.

The "wounded inner child" is a term used in psychology to refer to the emotional scars that people carry from childhood experiences that were traumatic, painful, or unmet needs (Davies, 2020). These experiences can cause the inner child to react in certain ways, such as with feelings of abandonment, fear, shame, and unworthiness. These behaviors can manifest in various ways, such as self-sabotage, addictive behaviors, or difficulty trusting others. Healing the hurt inner child means acknowledging these past events, learning to love and care for the inner child, and coming up with healthy ways to deal with triggers that can make you feel bad. With the help of therapy, support, and self-awareness, people can work towards healing their inner child and leading a more fulfilling life.

The early years of a child's life are crucial in shaping their emotional development. When a child is emotionally, psychologically, or physically neglected, they may learn to fear and feel abandoned in different ways. This can affect their emotional growth and their ability to form relationships in the future.

When a child's emotional needs—such as those for love, approval, or attention—are unmet by their caregivers, emotional neglect occurs. This can happen when parents are emotionally unavailable or preoccupied, leading the child to feel invisible or unimportant. As a result, the child may grow up feeling unworthy of love or affection and may struggle with intimacy and trust issues in their adult relationships.

When a child doesn't get the emotional and mental stimulation they need to grow up smart and emotionally healthy, psychological neglect is what happens. This can occur when a child is left alone for long periods of time. Children who experience psychological neglect may develop feelings of anxiety, low self-esteem, and depression.

Physical neglect means not meeting a child's physical needs, like giving them food, a place to sleep, clothes, and medical care. This can happen when caregivers are unable or unwilling to provide for the child's basic needs, resulting in feelings of insecurity and fear within the child. Children who aren't cared for physically may have trouble in their adult relationships with trust, regulating their emotions, and feeling safe.

These types of neglect can have a big effect on a child's emotional and mental health, creating fear and feelings of abandonment. To help the inner child heal and learn healthy ways to deal with problems, it is important to notice and deal with these problems as early as possible through therapy and support.

Because the concept of the inner child refers to the emotional and psychological experiences that people carry from their childhood into their adult lives, the inner child is believed to be the part of the psyche that retains the emotional memories and experiences of early life. Often manifesting in irrational fears, insecurities, and patterns of behavior later in life.

The age of reason is around seven years old, when children begin to develop a more logical and rational way of thinking. However, the inner child can begin to fear things long before the age of reason.

As children, we rely on our caregivers to meet our needs, and our brains are wired to detect potential threats in our environment. When our caregivers can't give us consistent care and support, or when we go through something traumatic, our brains may see these things as threats to our survival.

As a result, the inner child may begin to develop irrational fears and anxieties long before the logical mind has fully developed. These fears may be rooted in early experiences of abandonment, neglect, or abuse and can continue to impact our emotions and behaviors well into adulthood.

It is essential to recognize and address these early fears and traumas through therapy and self-awareness. By working to heal the wounded inner child, we can develop healthier emotional patterns and behaviors and build stronger, more fulfilling relationships with ourselves and others.

Does Modern Science Support the Inner Child's Early Conditioning to Fear and Insecurity and the Problems It Reveals in Your Adult Life?

Modern science says that a person's early experiences with fear and insecurity as a child can have a big effect on their lives as adults. Research in developmental psychology shows that children's subconscious minds absorb a great deal of information in the first six years of life, leading to long-lasting effects on emotional and psychological development.

During the sensitive period up to age six, children's brains are particularly susceptible to the information they receive from their environment. This time is very important for learning and development because this is when the brain makes neural connections that set the stage for how it will feel and think in the future.

This information is taken in and processed by the subconscious mind, which creates patterns of thought and behavior that may stay with a person well into adulthood. The analytical mind begins to develop between five and eight years old, and this is when the "inner child" is considered to be formed.

Between the ages of 8 and 12, the door between conscious

and subconscious thoughts closes, making it harder to reach the hurt inner child and heal it. This shows that early feelings of fear and insecurity can have an effect on a person's emotional and mental health for a long time.

Classical Conditioning vs. Operant Conditioning Theories

Classical conditioning is a type of learning where a stimulus, like a sound or smell, becomes associated with a certain response, while operant conditioning is a type of learning where behavior is shaped by consequences. Thus, classical conditioning is learning through association, while operant conditioning is learning through consequences.

Classical conditioning is a type of learning where a stimulus that doesn't naturally produce a response (a neutral stimulus) is repeatedly paired with a stimulus that does produce a response (an unconditioned stimulus), until the neutral stimulus alone begins to produce the same response (conditioned response).

Operant conditioning is a type of learning where behaviors are strengthened or weakened based on the consequences that follow them.

Now, let's talk about the fear response. When we experience a frightening event, our body goes into a fight-or-flight response, which is a natural survival mechanism. However, if that event is paired with a neutral stimulus, such as a sound or a place, our brain can learn to associate that neutral stimulus with fear, and we may begin to feel afraid or anxious in similar situations, even if there is no real threat.

This kind of conditioning can affect how we act and react for a long time, even as adults. It can also create emotional wounds in our inner child, as these experiences can shape our beliefs and perceptions about the world around us.

Children learn through their environment, which means that the subconscious mind absorbs information from the world around them during childhood. This information shapes their beliefs, values, and behaviors, and ultimately affects their mental and emotional health as adults (Dalien, 2015).

The environment that a child grows up in can have a profound impact on their inner child. The information that a child absorbs from their environment is stored in their subconscious mind. This information can be positive or negative, depending on the environment that the child grows up in. For example, if a child grows up in a home where they are encouraged to express their emotions and are provided with support and love, they are likely to have a healthy inner child. On the other hand, if a child grows up in a home where they are constantly criticized, neglected, or abused, they are more likely to have an unhealthy inner child.

The health of an inner child depends on what the environment fed it during childhood. So, it's important for parents and other caretakers to give children a safe and loving place to grow up. This will help them develop a healthy inner child that will serve them well throughout their lives.

According to experts (Foster & Brooks-Gunn, 2023), a child's community also plays a crucial role in conditioning their subconscious mind. The community includes the child's school, neighborhood, and wider social environment. These things can have a big influence on a child's cognitive, emotional, and social development, which ultimately shapes their personality and behavior.

For example, physical violence in the family or community can have a big effect on a child's growth and development. Violence can cause stress and trauma, which can make it difficult to make friends, to learn, and to build healthy relationships. Children who grow up in violent communities may also develop aggressive behavior.

On the other hand, a helpful and kind community can significantly aid in a child's development. A community that helps kids feel like they belong, gives them chances to learn and grow, and encourages healthy relationships can be good for their self-esteem and overall health. Children who grow up in such communities are more likely to develop positive social skills and attitudes.

A child's community also plays an important role in conditioning their subconscious mind. A supportive and positive community can contribute to a child's healthy development, while a violent or negative community can have negative effects on their mental and emotional health. Therefore, it is important for parents, caregivers, and community members to create a nurturing and safe environment for children to grow up in. This can help ensure that children develop a healthy and resilient inner self that will serve them well in their adult lives.

Piaget's Cognitive Development Theory

It is also possible that Piaget's cognitive development theory, particularly its emphasis on the sensorimotor, preoperational, and concrete-operational stages (Cherry, 2020), is another theory of childhood development that tends to favor poor inner child health.

Piaget's theory of cognitive development provides a framework for thinking about how kids' brains grow and change over time. Piaget proposed that children's minds develop in four distinct phases: the sensorimotor, the preoperational, the concrete-operational, and the formal-operational.

The first stage of cognitive development, known as the sensorimotor stage, typically occurs between the ages of 0 and 2. Infants at this age develop their senses and motor skills in preparation for later learning. They learn what psychologists call "object permanence," or the idea that things exist even when we can't see them. Infants also make simple mental pictures and learn to link what they feel with what they do with their bodies.

The preoperational stage is the second stage of cognitive

development, which typically lasts from around two to seven years old. During this stage, children begin to develop language and learn to use symbols to represent objects and ideas. They are also able to think about things that are not present and engage in pretend play. However, children at this stage struggle with conservation, which is the understanding that the quantity or shape of an object remains the same even if its appearance changes.

The concrete-operational stage is the third stage of cognitive development, which typically lasts from around seven to eleven years old. During this stage, children become more adept at using logic and mental operations. They are able to perform tasks that involve basic conservation and classification skills. They also begin to understand cause-and-effect relationships (Cherry, 2020).

Piaget's cognitive development theory is a good way to understand how children's cognitive abilities develop over time. By understanding these different stages, parents and educators can better support children's learning and development.

The Concept of Generational Trauma

Maybe you don't believe it's possible, but the truth is, trauma can be passed down from one generation to the next. Think of a mother who experienced severe trauma through the loss of her daughter. So, now her younger daughter was raised with great care and safety precautions in place, out of fear of losing her too. This resulted in the daughter being afraid of life. She eventually became a mom too; and when she had to raise her youngest of four, she felt the anxiety that something could happen to her baby, just like her mother feared something would happen to her. This caused the daughter to struggle with anxiety throughout her life. Because she never knew about her grandmother's or her own mother's trauma until much later in life, she never realized how it was related to her anxiety. Once she understood that her fears were rooted in the messages that her grandmother and mother fed her younger self, she could finally have the courage to break free from the fear mindset and pursue life with faith that everything will be okay, rather than fear that everything will go wrong.

You need to understand what generational trauma is to better grasp how your inner child suffers from the wounds they project from your behavior, thoughts, feelings, fears, and insecurities.

Generational trauma is a field of study where researchers are always learning more about how it affects people and how it shows up in their lives. Epigenetics is a new field of study that shows how trauma can be passed from one generation to the next through in-utero exposure or epigenetic changes. While much remains to be learned about epigenetics and inheritance patterns related to trauma, experts agree that generational trauma extends forward exponentially and can result in anxiety, depression, post-traumatic stress disorder (PTSD), and heightened traumatic reactivity. Everyone is susceptible to generational trauma, but populations vulnerable due to their histories include African Americans, families affected by natural disasters or catastrophes, and individuals who have experienced domestic violence, sexual assault, or abuse, and hate crimes. Generational trauma can show up as hypervigilance, a sense of a short future, mistrust, aloofness, high anxiety, depression, panic attacks, nightmares, insomnia, problems with self-esteem and self-confidence, and internalized oppression (Gillespie, 2020). Furthermore, trauma can alter the microglia and the immune system in ways that can be passed down through genetics. This theory is a psychological idea that has a lot in common with the Eastern model of the inner child. It says that rebirth and generational trauma from the past bring about rebirth in the present.

As you can see, your inner child isn't your fault. It gained its programming long before you could think with the conscious mind. Knowing and understanding this is the first priority to ensure you don't hold anything against your inner child. Working on your inner child won't be successful if you judge yourself. So, be kind and listen to what the voice tells you.

As a person thinks, feels, and believes, so is the condition of his mind, body, and circumstances. –Joseph Murphy

We need to understand that thoughts, beliefs, and emotions control everything in our life, including our circumstances. So, let's see what thoughts and beliefs are controlling your circumstances.

2

DISCERNMENT—IDENTIFYING THE
SOURCE OF YOUR WOUNDS

To heal the wounds of your past, you must first embrace your inner child with love, understanding, and compassion. Only then can you truly transform your habits and rewrite your story. - Unknown

The incident when I was four years old and left on the side of the road for a short while isn't the only abandonment issue I faced as a child. At six years old, my parents fought a lot, and I had an extreme fear that I would wake up and one of my parents would leave the home permanently. My parents eventually stopped fighting over the subject, and I no longer heard them yelling at each other in the middle of the night. Years later, when I was 13 years old, the same topic resurfaced, and my parents yelled at each other for a couple of months when I was a teenager. I was constantly afraid that my dad would leave us. Eventually, all the fighting stopped, and I left the home at age 18 to go to college and never heard them fight again because I only visited briefly over the holidays and d with them after I left and graduated college. Even hese fights were isolated incidents, their fighting affected my emotional state as a young teen, created a fear of abandonment, and fostered insecurities in me.

You are aware of the pain that was inflicted on your innocent inner child during your formative years, and you are not to blame. The next step is to learn how your subconscious processes affect your most fundamental convictions, sense of self-worth, and outlook on life. Healing one's inner child requires a focus on the self. You'll always carry a bit of your childhood with you (Sjöblom et al., 2016). So, isn't it time to change the story in your mind that will help you for the rest of your life? You can't change the story if you aren't paying attention to what it says.

Habitual Loops or Triggers

A habit loop or trigger is a three-step process that helps the brain develop and reinforce habits. Healthline (Raypole, 2021) says the habit loop is made up of a cue, a routine, and a reward.

The cue is the trigger that prompts the brain to initiate a specific behavior or habit. It could be something as simple as a particular time of day, a location, a feeling, or an event.

The routine is the actual behavior or habit that is performed in response to the cue. This could be a physical action, a thought pattern, or an emotional response.

The reward is the good result or feeling that comes after the routine is done. It reinforces the habit loop and motivates the brain to repeat the behavior in the future.

Understanding the habit loop can be helpful in changing unwanted habits or developing new, positive habits. By identifying the cue, individuals can consciously choose a new routine that leads to a desirable reward, and with repetition, a new habit can be formed.

Researchers did a study (Thomas et al., 2016) and the results showed that people can change their habit loops by changing their behavior on purpose. The research involved a group of participants who were asked to adopt a new exercise habit by practicing a specific behavior every day for 84 days. The participants reported on their own progress, and magnetic resonance imaging (MRI) was used to track changes in their brain activity.

The results showed that over time the participants were able to develop a new exercise habit that became automatic without requiring as much conscious effort as it did initially. The MRI data also showed that the participants' brain activity was changing, which indicated that their brains were getting used to the new habit loop. In particular, the researchers saw more activity in the basal ganglia, a part of the brain that helps form habits, and in the prefrontal cortex, a part of the brain that helps with planning and making decisions.

The study revealed that participants who successfully established the new exercise habit experienced positive changes in their overall wellbeing, including reduced stress levels and an improved mood. These results show that changing your behavior on purpose can change your habits in a way that lasts, which could be good for your physical and mental health.

From the above, it's evident that people can change their habit loops through deliberate behavior modification. By doing something new over and over again and letting your brain adjust, you can form a new habit that becomes automatic and helps your overall health.

Changing a habit loop requires deliberate and consistent effort, but it is possible with the right approach. Here are five steps you can follow:

1. **Identify the habit loop:** The first step is to identify the habit loop that you want to change. Habits

consist of three parts: the cue or trigger that initiates the behavior, the behavior itself, and the reward that reinforces the behavior. By understanding the components of your habit loop, you can start to disrupt the loop.

2. **Explore the triggers**: Once you have identified the habit loop, you need to explore the triggers that set it off. Triggers can be internal, such as emotions or thoughts, or external, such as people or situations. By understanding your triggers, you can start to anticipate them and plan alternative behaviors.

3. **Plan around the cues**: After identifying the triggers, the next step is to plan around the cues. If you want to change a habit, you need to replace the behavior with a new one that still satisfies the same cue. For example, if you tend to snack when you're stressed, you might try going for a walk or doing some stretching instead.

4. **Reward yourself**: Rewards play a crucial role in reinforcing habits, so it's essential to find alternative rewards that satisfy the same needs as the old habit. For example, if you used to reward yourself with a sugary treat, you might try rewarding yourself with a healthy snack or a fun activity instead.

5. **Be consistent**: Finally, to change a habit loop, you need to be consistent. Habits are formed through repetition, so it's important to practice your new behavior consistently until it becomes a new habit.

To change a habit loop, you need to figure out what the habit is, figure out what triggers it, plan alternative behaviors for cues, find alternative rewards, and practice the new behavior over and over again. With dedication and effort, anyone can change their habit loops and form new, healthier habits!

It is important to identify oneself in the process of behavior change. Behavior change is not just about changing actions or habits, it is also about changing one's identity. The way we identify ourselves determines the actions we take, and to create lasting behavior change, we must first change our identity (Eyal, 2022).

Identifying our inner child and its habits, thoughts, beliefs, and emotions helps us to understand our inner child, so we can begin to recognize the automatic habits and patterns that lead to unwanted circumstances. This can include behaviors like procrastination, overeating, or overspending. By identifying these patterns, we can begin to break free from them and make more intentional choices (Eyal, 2022).

Our beliefs about ourselves and the world around us shape our identity and influence our actions. By looking at our beliefs and values, we can start to figure out which ones might be holding us back or leading to bad habits.

Along with finding our inner child and looking at our beliefs and values, we should also be kind to ourselves. Changing behavior is not easy, and it's important to be kind to ourselves throughout the process. By acknowledging our successes and celebrating our progress, we can build momentum and stay motivated. So, how do you find yourself, your identity, or your inner child?

What Is the Self?

A person's self-concept is how they think about, judge, or see themselves. To know yourself is to have an idea of yourself (Mcleod, 2022).

Baumeister (1999) says that a person's self-concept is what

they think about themselves, including what qualities the person has and who or what the self is. Both social and humanistic psychology use the term "self-concept" a lot. Lewis (1990) says that there are two parts to the development of a sense of self:

The Self in Itself (Existential)

This is "the most basic part of the self-scheme or self-concept: the sense of being separate and different from others and the recognition of the constancy of the self" (Bee, 1992).

Are you ready to take charge of your mental health and the wellbeing of your relationships? Sign up now to get started on your way to being happier and healthier.

The child recognizes that they are different from everyone else and that they have always been there.

A child is aware of their existential self as early as two or three months old (Lewis, 1990). This is partly because of how the child interacts with the world. For instance, when the child smiles, someone smiles back; or when the child touches a mobile, it moves.

The Object of Self (Categorical)

After a child realizes that they are a separate being with feelings, they also realize that they are an object in the world.

Just as things, including people, have characteristics that can be experienced (big, small, red, smooth, etc.), the child is learning that they are also an object with characteristics that can be experienced.

Even the self can be put into groups based on things like age, gender, size, or skills. Age ("I'm three") and gender ("I'm a girl") are two of the first things that are used.

In early childhood, children put themselves in very clear categories (e.g., hair color, height, and favorite things). Later, people also start to talk about their own psychological traits, how they compare to others, and how other people see them.

The self-concept is made up of three parts (Rogers, 1959):

- How you feel about yourself (self-image).
- How much you think you're worth (self-esteem or self-worth).
- What you really wish you were like (ideal self).

How Does the Way You See Yourself Relate to Your Inner Child?

Self-image is how a person thinks and feels about themselves based on their experiences, emotions, and interactions with other people. This perception can be influenced by the "inner child," which refers to the child-like aspects of an individual's personality, including their feelings, thoughts, and behaviors, which have been carried forward from childhood. In this context, the inner child can impact an individual's self-image in various ways, including feelings of not being good enough, self-erasure, a lack of self-love and self-care, narcissistic tendencies, anxiety, and psychological dependency.

- **Not being good enough:** Individuals who struggle with their self-image and inner child frequently experience feelings of not being good enough. Hoffman (2018) says that this feeling often comes from being criticized, ignored, or abused as a child. These experiences can lead to the inner child believing that they are not worthy of love and attention, leading to a negative self-image in adulthood. People who think this way may be too hard on themselves and have unrealistic expectations that can lead to anxiety and low self-esteem.
- **Self-erasure:** According to Gartner (2016), self-erasure refers to the process of neglecting one's own

needs and desires to meet the expectations of others. Individuals who struggle with self-erasure often have a weak sense of self and may feel that their worth depends on their ability to please others. This behavior may stem from childhood experiences where the individual learned that their needs and desires were not important, leading to a negative self-image and a lack of self-love.

- **Lack of self-love and self-care:** As noted by Miller (2019), individuals who struggle with self-love and self-care may have learned from childhood experiences that they do not deserve to be taken care of, leading to a negative self-image and lack of self-esteem. This can manifest as a reluctance to prioritize self-care or engage in activities that promote self-love, leading to negative impacts on an individual's mental and physical health.
- **Narcissistic tendencies:** According to Aguirre and Galen (2017), individuals who struggle with narcissism often have a fragile self-image and a deep-seated fear of inadequacy. This fear may stem from childhood experiences where the individual did not receive adequate attention or validation, leading to a need for external validation in adulthood. Individuals with this perception may be excessively self-centered and lack empathy, leading to difficulties in relationships and negative impacts on their mental health.
- **Anxiety and psychological dependency:** According to Shapiro (2018), individuals who struggle with anxiety often have a negative self-image and a deep-seated fear of failure. This fear may stem from childhood experiences where the individual experienced criticism or punishment for mistakes,

leading to a sense of inadequacy and anxiety in
adulthood. Additionally, individuals who struggle
with psychological dependency may have learned
from childhood experiences that they need others to
meet their emotional needs, leading to negative
impacts on their mental health.

A person's self-image and their inner child are closely
linked, and both can have an effect on their mental health and
wellbeing in different ways. By understanding these connections and working to change any negative beliefs or actions,
people can boost their self-esteem, feel less anxious, and
improve their overall health.

How Neglect and Trauma Skew Our Self-Esteem

There are really only two types of problems with self-
esteem. Self-underestimation refers to a person's tendency to
give oneself a more negative evaluation than is warranted. It's
about feeling worthless, uncertain of oneself, doubting one's
own abilities, etc. The second kind is known as self-overestima-
tion and describes the propensity for an individual to think
highly of oneself when this is not the case. Superficiality, a false
sense of amplified self-worth, fakery, preoccupation with one's
social standing, and so on are all examples.

Let's discuss five challenges with self-esteem that many
individuals face. You may recognize some of these signs in
yourself, and you may have seen others in friends, family, and
acquaintances.

I'm Not Worthy

Many people feel like they are not good enough as children,
and this feeling sticks later in life. If we are mistreated as kids,
like we don't matter or aren't good enough, we might grow up
thinking we are never enough.

Most of the time, this kind of belief comes from being held

to standards that are too high (perfectionism), being compared to others, and being treated badly in general.

When we grow up with this kind of attitude, we start to think that nothing we do is good enough, that we can't relax, we have to do more, and many more things that aren't true.

Self-Deletion

People are often taught to take care of others and put their own needs, wants, preferences, feelings, and goals last. Many parents and caregivers, regardless of whether on purpose, see their child as somebody who should meet a lot of their needs (role reversal).

Because of all this, the child and the adult-child learn to give up on themselves and overlook their own needs. This leads to strong desires to please other people, poor self-care, a lack of purpose, emotional confusion, not even being able to say "no," and a detachment from oneself.

Not Caring for or Loving Oneself

Individuals who tend to undervalue themselves are often bad at taking care of themselves because they didn't get enough love and care as kids. Children who weren't properly cared for and didn't have good examples of self-loving, self-responsible, healthy caregivers often grow up to be adults who have trouble taking care of themselves (Cikanavicius, 2018).

So, this person now thinks, whether consciously or not, that they are not good enough to be loved or have their needs met. Sometimes it's because you don't know how to take care of yourself, but most of the time it's because you think you're not important enough, not worthy of love, can't have your needs met, or you don't matter.

An individual who thinks all of that is true will act in a way that is either self-neglectful or even self-destructive and self-sabotaging. Neglect in childhood results in neglect of oneself.

Narcissism in a Severe Form

Narcissists and psychopaths are often described as people

who have an exaggerated sense of their own importance. These traits span a broad range, although they have certain commonalities.

A highly narcissistic person is characterized by a number of traits, including insecurity, poor emotional regulation, black-and-white thinking, seeing everyone else as objects, superficial charm, self-absorption, manipulation, a relentless pursuit of attention, phoniness, confusion, inconsistency, pseudo-virtue, chronic lying, and a desire for social status and praise.

Narcissism and other poisonous personality characteristics are commonly learned defensive coping mechanisms in reaction to a stressful or traumatic upbringing.

Dependence on Others and Social Anxiety

Since other people have a big impact on us as we grow up, many of us become too worried about what other people think. This leads to many anxious views and feelings later in life, such as "What if they think I'm dumb?" "They think I look bad." "What can I do to win their favor?" "What if they think that I'm bad?" "I don't want to look like a wimp."

A large number of people depend on the approval and opinions of other people. They either try to get positive validation or stay away from negative and invalidating feedback. This mental dependence on other people causes a lot of social anxiety and often leads to bad behavior.

Having a healthy sense of self-worth is essential to our emotional and physical wellbeing. Our sense of who we are comes largely from the interactions we had with our parents and other major caregivers as children. Later, it expands to include other influential people, such as peers and superiors.

When we have an accurate perception of ourselves, we also have an appropriate sense of self-worth. When we're young, we tend to take on board the opinions of others and model our own identities after those impressions. Many people have a distorted sense of themselves in a variety of ways, which may lead to emotional, behavioral, and mental health issues.

We have the freedom and maturity to investigate how we see ourselves. In doing so, we may improve our sense of self-worth by eradicating the unhelpful and inaccurate beliefs we now have.

How Do Your Beliefs About Yourself, Others, and the World Around You Affect How You Feel and Think?

The model, which is the basis of cognitive-behavioral therapy (CBT), says that what you think about yourself has a big effect on your life. It changes how you treat other people, how you view the world, and how you think about your future. Your beliefs affect how you think, feel, and act.

Here's an example of how your beliefs can make a difference. Let's say you think, "I'm not good at anything." Now, let's say you're at work, and you just finished a task your boss gave you. Here's how your belief (I'm not good at what I do) will affect how you think:

- **Perception**: What you can see and feel. For example, your boss tells you that you did a poor job on the last task you were given. Since you think you're not good at what you do, you might sense that she's not satisfied with any of your work in general, and she thinks that you can't do anything right.
- **Attention**: What you decide to focus on. Since you think you're not good at what you do, you'll only pay attention to the criticism she just gave you and ignore the praise she gave you for things you've done in the past.
- **Memory**: What you know and what you remember. Since you think you're not good at what you do, it

will be easier for you to remember times when people in authority critiqued your job. Because of what you think, it will be harder for you to remember times when you felt good about what you were doing.

Our Thoughts Have a Huge Impact on Us

As you can see from the example above, what you think about yourself affects three parts of how you handle stress:

- How you see what's going on (perception).
- What you choose to focus on in the situation (attention).
- What you remember about the situation (memory).
- What you recall about all the other situations you've been in that are similar in some way.

Cognitive therapy teaches you how to question your thoughts so that you can see things in a more balanced and logical way. This is how it tries to get rid of these false and harmful beliefs. When you do this, you start to see yourself, your future, and other people in a healthier way.

Always keep in mind that you can change how you think, how you act, and how you feel. My goal is to give you some ideas about how to do this.

Your perceptions based on your beliefs determine how you respond to people, and it will outline your emotions after they respond to you. Your primal self or inner child became a fight-or-flight risk when you experienced too many negatives in classic conditioning, as one example of how your core beliefs turn into actions.

The Body's Stress Response

The Musculoskeletal System

Our musculoskeletal system, which consists of cartilage, bones, tendons, connective tissues, and ligaments, serves as our body's defense against pain and damage. Long-term muscular tension has the potential to cause various bodily responses and perhaps worsen stress-related diseases. Many individuals have chronic pain as a result of musculoskeletal diseases.

Stress has an impact on the musculoskeletal system as well since it causes muscles to tighten up and become stiff and tense for extended periods of time. Millions of people have debilitating chronic pain due to musculoskeletal diseases; therefore, it's crucial to maintain a certain amount of moderate, doctor-supervised exercise. Chronic, stress-related musculoskeletal problems are all facilitated by muscular tension, and ultimately, muscle atrophy as a result of body inactivity.

Our bodies can easily tolerate short bursts of stress, but prolonged or chronic stress may have negative repercussions. The immune, endocrine, gastrointestinal, neurological, and reproductive systems are just a few of the many bodily functions that can be negatively impacted by stress.

It has been shown that relaxation methods and other stress-relieving practices and treatments may successfully reduce muscular tension, lower the prevalence of certain stress-related illnesses, and boost feelings of wellbeing.

The Respiratory System

The respiratory system, which consists of your airway, lungs, and blood vessels, eliminates carbon dioxide waste from the body and delivers oxygen to cells. Air enters the body via the nose, travels down the trachea, through the larynx in the throat, then enters the lungs through the bronchi. Red blood cells are subsequently given oxygen by the bronchioles so they can circulate. Respiratory symptoms like shortness of breath and fast breathing may be an indication of stress and intense emotions. This is often not an issue for those without respiratory ailments, but for those with pre-existing respiratory conditions, like asthma and chronic obstructive pulmonary disease (COPD), psychological stresses may make breathing more difficult. An acute stressor, such as the loss of a loved one, may cause asthma episodes, and in those who are prone to panic attacks, it can also induce some acute episodes.

The Cardiovascular System

The cardiovascular system, consisting of your blood vessels and heart, works in tandem to provide the body's organs with nutrients and oxygen. Chronic stress may cause long-term issues with your heart and blood vessels. Your risk of hypertension, heart attacks, and stroke may increase as a result of this continuing stress. Recurrent acute stress and ongoing chronic stress may also lead to circulatory system inflammation, especially in the coronary arteries, and it seems that how someone handles stress might have an impact on their cholesterol levels.

Stress hormones serve as messengers for these effects during acute stress, which may result in an increase in heart rate and greater cardiac muscle contractions. Blood pressure rises as a result of the dilated arteries that provide blood to the heart, big muscles, and other major organs of the body. The body returns to normal when the acute stress experience has ended.

Chronic or persistent stress that lasts for a long time may damage the heart and blood vessels over the long run. This includes a faster heartbeat, higher blood pressure, and stress hormone levels, as well as circulatory system inflammation, especially in the coronary arteries. Depending on whether a woman is premenopausal or postmenopausal, she may be at a higher risk for heart disease. Estrogen levels are greater in premenopausal women, helping their blood arteries adapt more effectively to stress and defending them against heart disease. Due to their decreased estrogen levels, post-menopausal women are less protected against the effects of stress on heart disease.

The Endocrine System

The endocrine system consists of organs named glands that produce hormones in your body. Chronic stress may cause compromised immune system and HPA axis communication, which can result in physical and mental health disorders. The endocrine system (including glucocorticoids like cortisol) is in charge of controlling the immune system and lowering inflammation. The pituitary gland is signaled by the hypothalamus, a group of nuclei that links the brain and the endocrine system, to generate a hormone, which is subsequently signaled to the adrenal glands to enhance cortisol production. By releasing glucose and fatty acids from the liver, cortisol increases the amount of energy fuel that is readily accessible.

Stress and Your Health

Early-life stress may alter how the neurological system develops and how the body responds to stress. Many physical and mental health issues, such as chronic tiredness, metabolic abnormalities, depression, and immunological diseases, have been related to stress. Stress may impact the brain-gut connection, affecting your mental health, which can further influence the hundreds of millions of relatively autonomous gut neurons that communicate constantly with the brain and cause pain, bloating, and other gut discomfort. Gut bacterial alterations brought on by stress may have an impact on mood. It's an unhealthy circle that won't stop affecting your health unless you take control of your stress levels.

The Gastrointestinal System

Like I explained, early-life stress may alter how the neurological system develops as well as how the body responds to stress, which might raise the likelihood of developing gastrointestinal disorders or malfunction in the future.

The digestive system is very big because it contains the mouth, throat, esophagus, stomach, small and large intestines, rectum, and anus. Further, it contains the salivary glands, gall-bladder, pancreas, and liver, which make enzymes and digestive juices that help the body break down food and fluids.

Stress may unnecessarily increase or reduce appetite, as well as make pain, bloating, nausea, and other stomach symptoms easier to feel.

Stress may also cause muscular spasms in the intestine, which can be uncomfortable and make it easier to feel pain, bloating, or discomfort there. Stress may impact digestion and the nutrients that are absorbed by the intestines, which can lead to an increase in gas linked to nutrition absorption. The intestines contain a strong barrier that prevents germs from the gut from entering the body via food, but stress may damage this barrier. Particularly in those with persistent gastrointestinal issues, this may result in moderate, long-lasting symptoms.

Heartburn or acid reflux may be brought on by eating more or less than usual. Stress may impair nutrition absorption and digestion, which might result in recurrent yet mild symptoms. Stress may also have an impact on the neurological system.

The Nervous Systems

The brain and spinal cord make up the central part of the nervous system. The autonomic and somatic nervous systems make up the peripheral part of the nervous system (APA, 2018; Cherry, 2022).

The sympathetic nervous system (SNS) and the parasympathetic nervous system (PNS) are parts of the autonomic nervous system (ANS). The sympathetic nervous system is in charge of how the body reacts to stress. When the body is under a lot of stress, the SNS helps trigger the fight-or-flight response. The body shifts its energy to fight off a threat to its life or run away from an intruder (APA, 2018; Cherry, 2022).

The SNS tells the adrenal glands to release the hormones

cortisol and adrenaline. In an emergency, these hormones and the direct actions of autonomic nerves cause the heart to beat faster, the breathing rate to increase, the blood vessels in the arms and legs to widen, the digestive process to change, and the amount of glucose (sugar energy) in the bloodstream to rise.

The SNS response happens pretty quickly, so the body is ready to deal with an emergency or a short-term source of stress. Once the emergency is over, the body normally goes back to how it was before the emergency. This recovery is helped by the PNS, which has effects that are usually the opposite of the SNS. But PNS overactivity can also cause stress reactions, like making the airways narrower (as in asthma) or making the blood vessels dilate too much and reducing blood flow (APA, 2018).

Both the SNS and the PNS have strong connections with the immune response, which can also regulate stress reactions. The autonomic nervous system is regulated by the central nervous system (CNS), and the ANS is a big part of how the CNS decides if a situation is potentially dangerous.

Chronic stress, which is caused by stressors that last for a long time, can drain the body over time. As long as the autonomic nervous system keeps causing physical responses, it wears down the body. It's not so much about how chronic stress affects the nervous system that's a problem, but what it does to other parts of the body when the nervous system is always on (APA, 2018).

The Male Reproductive System

The autonomic nervous system, which produces testosterone and activates the sympathetic nervous system, has an impact on the male reproductive system (APA, 2018). The hormone, cortisol, which is vital for controlling blood pressure and the regular operation of various bodily systems, is released by stress on the body. The male reproductive system, sperm production and maturation, sperm disorders, and the normal biochemical functioning of the male reproductive system may all be impacted by excessive cortisol levels. Moreover, it may have a detrimental effect on the development and synthesis of testosterone, making it more difficult for couples to conceive. Normal male reproductive function may be impacted by diseases of the reproductive system, such as infections of the testes, prostate, and urethra.

The Female Reproductive System

During the course of their lives, women balance a wide variety of responsibilities, including those related to their personal lives, families, careers, finances, and other obligations, in addition to health care issues. Teenage girls' and women's menstruation may be impacted by stress, which has been linked to shorter or non-existent menstrual cycles, painful periods, and variations in cycle duration. Premenstrual syndrome (PMS), which includes symptoms such as cramps, bloating from fluid retention, an irritated attitude, and mood swings, may be unpleasant for many women (APA, 2018).

A woman's intentions for having children might be significantly impacted because stress during pregnancy may have a detrimental effect on a woman's ability to conceive, the health of her pregnancy, and her capacity to adapt after giving birth. The most common pregnancy and postpartum adjustment issue is depression, and a mother's stress may have a severe influence on fetal and continuing childhood development (APA, 2018).

Although hormone levels vary vastly and physical changes like hot flashes may be difficult to deal with, menopause itself can be stressful. Stress may also be brought on by conditions that affect the reproductive system, such as polycystic ovarian syndrome or the herpes simplex virus (APA, 2018).

Menopause may be stressful because hormone levels change quickly and dealing with the physical changes related to menopause can be challenging. Reproductive system disorders may lead to a lot of stress, which calls for extra care and assistance.

These findings about how stress affects health shouldn't cause you to worry. We now know a lot more about how to reduce stress responses in a healthy way than in earlier years. Among these helpful strategies are:

- keeping a strong network of friends and family
- doing physical activity on a regular basis
- getting a good night's sleep every night

These approaches focus on both your physical and mental health and are important parts of a healthy way of life. You need to figure out the problems and stressors that impact your daily life and find the best ways to deal with them to improve your physical and mental health as a whole.

How Do You Create a Better Self-Concept?

Sometimes I'll recommend that my adult followers treat their "inner child" with the same awe, compassion, and patience that they'd shown their own kid or any other youngster that came across as vulnerable. I would like to recommend that they consider themselves with the admiration and respect that we give a beautiful baby at birth, ready to grow in the best possible manner, and ask for forgiveness for whatever imagined wrong-doings they may have committed in the past.

Your beliefs and inner child's automatic behavior also isn't your fault. It's an automatic system you need to switch off to heal the inner child. Understanding the principles of how the inner child's automatic system works can help you identify the cues and responses to change habit loops and triggers.

We are what we repeatedly do. Excellence, then, is not an act, but a habit. –Will Durant

With the half-technical support of science behind your inner child's automatic workings, it's time to call out to the seat of your mind, listening to its troubles, extending a helpful hand, and finding ways to heal this beautiful inner child.

3

CALLING OUT THE INNER CHILD AND LISTENING TO WHAT IT SCREAMS

R ecognizing underlying beliefs that impact how you think, feel, and act around yourself and others is a great place to start before discovering the three stages to healing your inner child. Hence, instead of dismissing the inner child's screams, stop rejecting its instinctive answers to pinpoint the specific difficulties in your life.

Did you know that your inner child's voice may make you feel powerless and 10 times worse than before? Turning up your inner child's voice can help you find numerous erroneous ideas that cause you to feel the way you do.

What Is Your Inner Child's Voice?

Self-talk is the automatic dialogue inside your subconscious mind. Your younger version within you tells you what it believes from its own experiences including hurt, rejection, and shame. Consider what you've spoken to yourself today for a moment. What did you tell yourself? Let's be honest now. Were you cruel, or were you helpful and kind? How did you feel after talking with yourself about this? Your emotions and mood are caused by your thoughts. Conversations with oneself may be destructive.

Self-talk is a behavior you engage in spontaneously throughout the day. Positive self-talk is becoming more popular as a strong method for developing self-confidence and reducing negative feelings. Positive self-talk masters are regarded to be more confident, driven, and productive.

Although some people are born with good self-talk, the majority of people must learn how to foster happy ideas and dispel negative ones. It might become more instinctual to entertain pleasant ideas rather than harmful ones with practice.

Positive Self-Talk vs. Negative Self-Talk

Positive self-talk is encouraging and reassuring. Examine the two inner assertions below:

- Today, I'm going to speak up at the meeting as I have something essential to say. This appears to be a positive strategy and attitude.
- I'm not sure I want to speak up at the meeting today since I'll appear stupid if I say something foolish.

Contrast this unfavorable comment with the preceding statement. Quite self-destructive, right?

The opposite of positive self-talk is ruminating. It occurs when you constantly replay painful or cringe-worthy ideas or experiences in your mind. Thinking over a problem might be beneficial, but if you devote excessive time to pondering, minor difficulties tend to worsen. Rumination might increase your chances of developing sadness or anxiety.

What Is Negative Self-Talk? How Can It Affect You?

Welcome to your inner critic. Your own worst enemy. Self-critique may take many forms. There are both practical and cruel interpretations: *I'm not good at this, so I should avoid doing it for my own physical safety*, for example. You may think that you're making a fair evaluation of the situation, like: *I got a D on this test. My low math grades have made me fear that I would never be able to attend a prominent university.*

The inner critic might remind you of a previous critic in your life, such as a parent or acquaintance. Possible outcomes include catastrophizing, condemning, and other related cognitive mistakes.

The effects of destructive internal dialogue can be far reaching. Large-scale research has connected negative events ruminating and self-blame to an elevated likelihood of developing psychological disorders.

Negative thinking has been linked to a loss of drive and an increase in hopelessness. Depression has been connected to this kind of self-criticism; therefore, it's clear that it has to be addressed.

Negative self-talk can make it harder to see possibilities and less likely to take advantage of them when they come up. This means that the increased sense of anxiety comes from both how it is perceived and how it causes people to act. Negative self-talk can also have the following destructive effects:

- **Thinking small**: When you tell yourself over and over that you can't do something, you start to believe it.
- **Perfectionism**: You start to believe that "great" isn't as nice as "perfect" and that you can reach perfection. On the other hand, people who don't try to be flawless tend to do better than those who do because they are less stressed and pleased with a job well done. They don't try to figure out what could have been done better.

- **Feeling depressed:** Having negative thoughts about yourself can make you feel even worse. If nothing is done, this could be very destructive.
- **Challenging relationships:** Whether your continuous self-judgment makes you seem emotional and unconfident, or you turn your negative self-talk into more general negative routines that trouble others, a communication gap and also a "light-hearted" level of criticism can create strain on your personal and work relationships.

One of the most glaring problems with self-criticism is that it doesn't make you feel better. People who talk to themselves positively, frequently experience more positive results. Yes, self-encouragement is a predictor of success. So, go on, tell yourself that you are busy doing something great, and others will soon notice it too.

Can Positive Self-Talk Change Your Life?

You may change your internal conversation if you feel it's too negative or if you want to put more emphasis on good thoughts. It has the potential to make you a happier and healthier person.

Positive self-talk has been shown to increase productivity and wellbeing. More optimistic thinking and self-talk has been linked to several therapeutic benefits, such as:

- improved health
- increased happiness
- strengthened defenses
- improved cardiovascular health and decreased discomfort
- increased happiness and contentment
- decreased mortality risk

- improved physical health

It is unclear why those who are more optimistic and who engage in more positive self-talk gain these advantages. According to Holland (2018), research reveals that those who engage in positive self-talk may have the mental abilities that make it easier for them to solve issues, think creatively, and deal well with adversity. The negative consequences of stress and anxiety may be mitigated in this way.

Taking Your Inner Voice Seriously

The inner child's thoughts and beliefs can be investigated through an individual's self-talk. Thus, it's a method to see how your deepest convictions are influencing your life. Next, you must identify the common signs of how your inner child behaves beyond the critical self-talk stemming from your automatic dialogue. When someone acts in a specific way, it's easy to see that their inner child is hurting.

Below are several behaviors indicative of a damaged inner child, with or without the accompanying inner monologue:

- **Reacting over-emotionally about small things:** How do you know you have emotional scars from your childhood if some of them occurred when you were too little to recall them? One technique is to examine your reactions to circumstances for hints, especially if any of them appear exaggerated. You may have unfulfilled requirements for attention as a youngster if, for instance, you become really furious when a friend glances at their phone while you are talking to them.
- **Practicing self-sabotage:** The term "self-sabotaging conduct" is used to describe any action (or lack

thereof) taken with the specific aim to sabotage one's own efforts. Self-sabotaging behavior on my part included, for instance, starting pointless arguments with my ex-spouse about trivial matters.

- **Toxic coping methods**: One way to deal with tough feelings is by employing a coping method. Those who suffered trauma as children may later turn to unhealthy coping mechanisms, like substance abuse, excessive drinking, or immersing themselves too deeply in virtual worlds, such as video games and social media. They may also overextend themselves in an effort to avoid dealing with their emotions.

- **Experiencing difficulties in close, personal relationships**: This might involve familial difficulties, feeling rejected, feeling chastised, feeling like an outsider, or a significant emotional reliance between you and a parent. Whatever the situation, any form of hard family ties can be pointing to old, unresolved childhood issues and unmet needs.

- **Consistently retaining poor self-esteem and blaming yourself**: Being raised by highly critical or demanding individuals can lead to the development of an inner critic who constantly finds fault and nullifies one's emotions.

- **Issues with toxic relationships**: If you repeatedly choose partners who make you sad or who are inaccessible, it may be a sign that your ability to form healthy connections with others may have been severely damaged as a youngster.

- **Persistent mental health problems, including depression and anxiety**: Those who have suffered an inner childhood wound may struggle with emotions of emptiness, powerlessness, and despair on a regular basis. They may worry that they are only a shell of their true selves and that their existence is devoid of any passion or originality. For example, they may feel alone and isolated, while being surrounded by people.

- **Abandonment:** Those who have experienced neglect, rejection, or abandonment in the past may be more susceptible to developing a phobia of being left alone or abandoned in both the physical and emotional worlds. Neglect, abuse, or the death of a loved one can all fall into this category. A person's relationships, beliefs, emotions, and conduct can all be negatively impacted by abandonment issues. The "inner child" of a person might be unhappily affected by abandonment concerns. Relational clinginess, jealousy, possessiveness, feelings of insecurity, and poor self-worth are all examples of abandonment difficulties.

- **Rejection fear:** Anxiety, insecurity, and poor self-esteem can all result from the fear of rejection, which is a frequent emotional response to the risk of being rejected or excluded by others. If you're afraid of being rejected, you might never ask someone out for dinner or tell them how you feel. Negative self-beliefs, such as "I'm not good enough" or "I don't deserve love," might form when a person's inner child encounters rejection or isolation. Because of this, the individual may begin to doubt their own value and ruin their relationships in an effort to prevent further rejection.

- **Lacking the courage to speak up and share your thoughts and feelings:** This concept pertains to the fear of expressing oneself, setting boundaries, or asserting their opinions due to the fear of being rejected or facing negative consequences. For instance, if an individual feels uncomfortable in a situation but fails to speak up, it may cause resentment or anger towards themselves or others. This fear can impact their inner child by stopping them from expressing their needs and desires, leading to a feeling of emotional neglect or pain.

- **No confidence in others:** This concept is centered around the lack of trust in others, which can be due to past experiences of betrayal or trauma. For instance, a person who has been lied to or cheated on may find it hard to trust others in future relationships. This lack of trust can affect their inner child by creating feelings of insecurity and fear, making them feel unsafe or unimportant in their relationships.

- **Driven by a desire to please people:** This concept describes the inclination to prioritize other people's needs and desires over one's own, often at the cost of their own happiness and wellbeing. For example, an individual who always says yes to others' requests but ignores their own needs may feel overwhelmed or resentful. This behavior can impact their inner child by creating feelings of inadequacy or low self-esteem, leading to a belief that their own needs are unimportant or not valued.

- **Allowing others to cross your boundaries:** This refers to the tendency of allowing others to violate your personal space, values, and beliefs, leading to a feeling of resentment, low self-worth, and powerlessness. For example, if a person fails to set boundaries with an abusive partner, they may develop feelings of shame or guilt, which can impact

their inner child by creating feelings of
unworthiness and neglect.

- **Inclination towards addictive behaviors:** This
refers to the tendency to engage in excessive and
compulsive behaviors, such as substance abuse or
gambling, leading to a feeling of loss of control and
negative consequences. For instance, a person who
abuses drugs may feel trapped and unable to stop,
leading to feelings of self-loathing and despair. This
behavior can impact their inner child by creating
feelings of shame, guilt, and a belief that they are
not worthy of love and support.

- **Avoiding people:** This refers to the tendency of
avoiding social situations, leading to a feeling of
loneliness, isolation, and difficulty in forming
connections with others. For example, a person who
avoids social gatherings may feel left out or
disconnected, which can impact their inner child by
creating feelings of sadness, insecurity, and a belief
that they are not worthy of belonging and acceptance.

- **Quick to anger:** This refers to the tendency to
become angry or irritable quickly, leading to a
feeling of losing control, frustration, and difficulty in
managing emotions. For instance, a person who gets
angry quickly may lash out at others, leading to
feelings of guilt or regret. This behavior can impact
their inner child by creating feelings of insecurity,
unworthiness, and a belief that they are not capable
of handling situations effectively.

- **Difficulty with letting go:** This concept refers to the
tendency to hold onto negative thoughts, emotions,
or experiences, leading to a feeling of being stuck or
trapped. For example, a person who cannot let go of

a past relationship may constantly replay the events and feel stuck in the pain, which can impact their inner child by creating feelings of unworthiness and low self-esteem.

- **Fear of new things:** This concept refers to the tendency to feel anxious or scared of unfamiliar situations or experiences, leading to a feeling of being unable to cope or adapt. For example, a person who is afraid to try new things may miss out on opportunities for growth and development, leading to feelings of regret and self-doubt. This behavior can impact their inner child by creating feelings of insecurity, fear, and a belief that they are not capable of handling new experiences.

- **Perfectionism:** This concept refers to the tendency to strive for perfection in all aspects of life, leading to a feeling of pressure and self-criticism. For example, a person who is a perfectionist may feel anxious and stressed when they cannot achieve their goals or standards, leading to feelings of inadequacy and low self-esteem. This behavior can impact their inner child by creating feelings of self-doubt, shame, and a belief that they are not good enough.

- **Feeling like you did something wrong all the time:** This concept refers to the tendency to feel guilty or ashamed about one's actions or thoughts, leading to a feeling of self-blame and unworthiness. For example, a person who feels like a sinner may constantly criticize themselves and feel unworthy of love and forgiveness, leading to feelings of isolation and despair. This behavior can impact their inner child by creating feelings of shame, self-hatred, and a belief that they are not worthy of love and acceptance.

- **Expecting failure:** This concept refers to the tendency to anticipate negative outcomes or experiences, leading to a feeling of hopelessness and helplessness. For example, a person who expects failure may give up on their goals or dreams before even trying, leading to feelings of regret and self-doubt. This behavior can impact their inner child by creating feelings of low self-worth, fear, and a belief that they are not capable of achieving their goals.

- **Seeking abusive partners:** This concept refers to the tendency to seek out relationships that are harmful or abusive, leading to a feeling of being trapped or unable to escape. For example, a person who seeks abusive partners may believe that they deserve to be treated poorly or that they cannot find anyone else, leading to feelings of low self-worth and self-blame. This behavior can impact their inner child by creating feelings of insecurity, fear, and a belief that they are not deserving of healthy and loving relationships.

- **Feeling like you don't fit in:** This concept refers to the tendency to feel like an outsider or to struggle with fitting in with others, leading to a feeling of loneliness and isolation. For example, a person who feels like they don't fit in may struggle to make friends or form connections with others, leading to feelings of rejection and self-doubt. This behavior can impact their inner child by creating feelings of inadequacy, low self-esteem, and a belief that they are not worthy of belonging and acceptance.

- **Clingy or being a loner:** This concept refers to the tendency to either cling onto others or to isolate oneself from others, leading to a feeling of being unable to form healthy relationships. For example, a person who is clingy may feel anxious and needy in their relationships, leading to feelings of rejection and abandonment when they don't receive the desired level of attention. Similarly, a person who is a complete loner may feel disconnected and isolated from others, leading to feelings of loneliness and inadequacy, which can impact their inner child by creating a belief that they are not lovable or worthy of connection.

- **Can't stand your ground:** This concept refers to the difficulty in asserting oneself, setting boundaries, or expressing opinions, leading to a feeling of powerlessness, resentment, and difficulty in building healthy relationships. For example, a person who can't stand their ground may feel overwhelmed or anxious in situations where they need to assert themselves, leading to feelings of regret or frustration when they fail to do so. This behavior can impact their inner child by creating a belief that they are not capable or deserving of standing up for themselves, leading to a feeling of inadequacy or low self-esteem.

Discover what hurt you as a child, so you can fully understand what to do next and make changes. This will also help you set goals, break bad habits, and use the right affirmations and mantras when you meditate and heal your chakras.

Questionnaire: Is Your Inner Child Wounded?

Below is a simple questionnaire you can complete to help identify if your inner child is wounded.

1. Do you still hold onto bitterness and anger from things that happened when you were young?

- Yes
- No

1. Were you able to be your true self when you were young?

- Yes
- No

1. How do you remember your childhood?

- Not that great
- An amazing experience

1. If you had the chance, would you like to go back to your childhood?

- Not at all
- Yes, definitely

1. Do you find it hard to stand and speak up for yourself?

- Yes
- No

1. Do you get nervous around people? Social anxiety?

- Yes
- No

1. Do you find it hard to handle your feelings?

- Yes
- No

1. Do you fear that someone will abandon you?

- Yes
- No

1. Do you have problems with trusting others?

- Yes
- No

1. Have you ever used alcohol, cigarettes, or even shopping, to forget about something bad that happened in the past?

- Yes
- No

1. Do you often get self-conflicted or involved in conflict with others?

- Yes
- No

12. Do you often blame others for your mistakes?

- Yes
- No

How many of the above questions have you answered that

correlate with the signs of a wounded child? Self-evaluate based on your answers. This will guide you on which aspects you need to work on and overcome.

The wounded inner child is the primary gateway to healing and integration. –Marcus W. Kasunich

Great, you're listening to your inner child's voice now, but let's discover how the inner child can influence your life, well-being, and relationships before piloting the steps to healing an inner child.

4

HOW YOUR INNER CHILD CRIES OUT

Sometimes, you have to see how the wounds of your inner child impact your wellbeing, happiness, connections, finances, and other small details before you can fully understand how important it is to heal before things become worse. So, let's find out how the state of your inner child affects every aspect of your everyday life. Even if you find out the truth about your core beliefs, they can stay the same. So, putting your plan into action may not work until you know what will happen if you don't. It's difficult to confront the truths about who we have become and what we do, but meditation and chakra healing can help you have a magical experience, when you do.

We unknowingly look to our relationships, jobs, and the outside world to *solve* problems we had as young children. We turn to others to meet our spiritual, emotional, and physical needs that we didn't get at home or that came at a price when we were young. Of course, you can't expect that to happen. After all, we *project* on other people what we had hoped for from our parents in the first place instead of looking into what hurt us. It was the first idea that someone would take care of us because we couldn't. Fears about being capable of survival in *these times* bring back the pain from the beginning. Maybe it's happening now for a reason. Now might be a good time to look into it.

How Do Your Inner Child's Wounds Affect Your Happiness?

The emotional wounds we may have experienced during childhood can include neglect, rejection, abandonment, and abuse, among others. When our inner child's wounds are not properly healed, they can continue to affect us in our adult lives. These wounds can manifest in various ways, including low self-esteem, anxiety, depression, and a lack of trust in others. These negative emotions can lead to a reduced sense of happiness and wellbeing.

For example, if someone experienced rejection or neglect as a child, they may develop a deep-seated fear of abandonment as an adult. This fear can prevent them from forming close relationships or trusting others, which can lead to feelings of isolation and loneliness.

Similarly, if someone experienced abuse as a child, they may struggle with low self-esteem and feelings of worthlessness. These negative beliefs can continue to impact their adult life, making it difficult for them to assert themselves or pursue their goals.

To address these inner child wounds, it is important to engage in healing practices that help to process and release the pain and emotions associated with past experiences. This can include therapy, mindfulness practices, and self-care activities that nurture the inner child and help to build self-compassion and self-love.

Ultimately, healing our inner child's wounds can help us to experience greater happiness and fulfillment in our adult lives, as we learn to let go of negative beliefs and emotions and embrace a sense of inner peace and wellbeing. Mental stability is the source of long-term happiness. So, healing your inner child's wounds can make you feel much happier for much longer, and you won't have to find a "quick fix" that will only make you forget for a short while, and harm you in the long run.

How Do Your Inner Child's Wounds Affect Your Finances?

Your wounded inner child can create self-sabotaging behaviors, like overspending, missing bills, and treating yourself with expensive gifts for quick-fix emotional shots of dopamine and serotonin.

Our inner child's wounds can have a significant impact on our financial behaviors and decisions as adults. When we experience emotional wounds during childhood, such as neglect, abandonment, or abuse, we may develop coping mechanisms that manifest as self-sabotaging behaviors in our financial lives.

For example, someone who experienced neglect as a child may feel a constant sense of scarcity and anxiety around money as an adult. This may lead them to overspend, hoard money, or have difficulty managing their finances.

Similarly, someone who experienced abuse as a child may have developed a pattern of seeking out material possessions as a way to cope with emotional pain. They may engage in impulsive spending or treat themselves to expensive gifts as a way to seek a temporary sense of comfort or validation.

These self-sabotaging behaviors can have long-term consequences on our financial stability and wellbeing. Overspending or missing bills can lead to debt and financial stress, while relying on material possessions for emotional fulfillment can lead to a never-ending cycle of consumerism and financial insecurity.

To address these behaviors, it is important to recognize and heal our inner child's wounds. This can involve working with a therapist or counselor to address the emotional pain and develop healthy coping mechanisms, as well as practicing mindfulness and self-care activities to build self-awareness and self-compassion.

It is also helpful to develop a financial plan and budget that aligns with our values and long-term goals, as this can provide a sense of stability and direction in our financial lives. By addressing our inner child's wounds and developing healthy financial habits, we can achieve greater financial stability and wellbeing and break free from self-sabotaging behaviors that keep us stuck in cycles of stress and insecurity.

How Does a Wounded Inner Child Affect Relationships?

Our wounded inner child can have a significant impact on our ability to form and maintain healthy relationships. When we carry unresolved emotional wounds from childhood, we may struggle with trust, intimacy, and emotional connection, which can impact our relationship energy and motivation from the start.

A wounded inner child may also cause us to crave a sense of belonging and acceptance, which can make us vulnerable to abusive relationships. This is because we may be willing to overlook red flags or tolerate mistreatment to feel loved and accepted. This can perpetuate a cycle of emotional pain and trauma that can impact our wellbeing and future relationships.

Moreover, our wounded inner child can cause us to become unintentionally manipulative, ruining potentially good relationships. This can happen when we try to control our partner or avoid vulnerability out of fear of being rejected or hurt. These manipulative behaviors can cause our partners to feel disrespected or disregarded, leading to relationship break-downs and emotional pain.

To address our wounded inner child and improve our relationships, it is important to seek healing and support. This can involve working with a therapist or counselor to address our emotional wounds and develop healthy coping mechanisms, as well as practicing self-care activities to build self-awareness and self-compassion.

It's important to establish clear boundaries and expectations in our relationships, and to communicate openly and honestly with our partners. By addressing our inner child's wounds and developing healthy relationship skills, we can form and maintain fulfilling, mutually supportive relationships that contribute to our overall wellbeing and happiness.

When we carry unresolved emotional wounds from childhood, we may struggle with forming and maintaining healthy relationships. This can result in a range of behavioral consequences that can further sabotage any potentially healthy relationships.

One of these consequences is jealousy, which can stem from a fear of losing the love and acceptance of our partner. This can lead to controlling behavior, such as constantly checking their phone or social media accounts, which can ultimately lead to conflict in the relationship.

Clinginess can also be a result of a wounded inner child, as we may feel a constant need for validation and attention from our partner. This can cause us to put our partner ahead of ourselves, leading to a lack of personal boundaries and self-betrayal.

Furthermore, a fear of abandonment and rejection can lead to codependency, which can further sabotage relationships. This can cause us to stay in incompatible or abusive relationships, as we fear being alone or rejected.

A fear of commitment, vulnerability, and intimacy can also

be a consequence of a wounded inner child, as we may feel a sense of discomfort or anxiety around these aspects of relationships. This can lead to a lack of sexual and personal boundaries, as well as a feeling of shame around our bodies and selves. A tendency to put others' needs ahead of our own and struggling with trust, a history of codependency, and finding ourselves repeating patterns in relationships are other signs of a wounded inner child.

Unhealthy relationships are a bad cycle that wounds the inner child further. In addition, abusive and toxic relationships are more common as you feel attached to people who abuse, avoid, or neglect you because you believe it's normal. Relationships include any and all, such as family, friends, and romantic partners.

Some common signs of an unhealthy relationship include:

- lack of communication or poor communication
- controlling behavior or manipulation
- constant criticism or put-downs
- feeling unsupported or neglected
- physical or emotional abuse
- lack of trust or jealousy
- consistent conflict or arguing
- ignoring boundaries or violating personal space
- isolation from friends or family
- feeling unhappy, anxious, or depressed around the other person

It's important to note that every relationship is unique and what works for one person may not work for another. However, if you are experiencing any of these signs in your relationship, it's important to address them and seek support. This can involve talking openly and honestly with your partner, seeking counseling or therapy, or even ending the relationship if it's not healthy or fulfilling. Remember that you deserve to be in a relationship that brings you joy, happiness, and support.

How Does a Wounded Inner Child Affect Your Career?

The repetition compulsion cycle impacts our careers by causing us to unconsciously repeat past experiences and patterns to fix unresolved emotions and traumas. These patterns often stem from childhood experiences and can result in choosing a career that mirrors past experiences or struggling to make progress in our careers due to emotional issues. This can be harmful as our careers significantly impact our wellbeing. Workaholism can also be a way of coping with past emotional wounds and trauma, often linked to childhood experiences, such as neglect or emotional abuse. While the drive to succeed can be positive, harmful work habits can lead to stress and burnout. To address these issues, it's important to explore the root causes of our behavior, learn healthy coping mechanisms, set boundaries and priorities, and achieve a more balanced approach to our careers and lives. It may also involve setting clear boundaries and priorities to ensure that we are balancing work with other aspects of our lives, such as hobbies, relationships, and self-care.

By addressing the underlying emotional wounds, developing healthy habits, and coping mechanisms, we can break free from work addiction and achieve a healthier, more balanced approach to our careers and lives.

Your career is influenced heavily by your inner child, and you might be allowing everyone to take advantage of you in the endless pursuit of perfection and validation! You can't be happy in such work circumstances.

How Do the Inner Child's Wounds Influence Your Parenting?

The wounds of your inner child can have a significant impact on your parenting style and abilities. The way that you were raised and the emotional wounds that you experienced as a child can shape the way that you approach parenting and interact with your own children.

If you experienced neglect or emotional abuse as a child, you may struggle to provide your children with the love, care, and attention that they need. You may have difficulty setting healthy boundaries, managing your own emotions, or responding effectively to your children's needs.

On the other hand, if you experienced overprotective or controlling parenting, you may inadvertently replicate these patterns with your own children. You may struggle to give your children the space and freedom that they need to grow and develop, or you may be overly critical or demanding of their behavior and achievements.

Your inner child's wounds can also affect the way that you cope with stress and manage conflict with your children. If you experienced trauma or emotional pain as a child, you may have difficulty regulating your own emotions and responding calmly to your children's behavior. You may also struggle to communicate effectively or establish a healthy sense of trust and security with your children.

However, becoming aware of these patterns and working to heal your own emotional wounds can help you become a more effective and nurturing parent. Seeking support from a therapist or counselor can help you identify the areas where you struggle and develop healthy coping mechanisms and communication skills to better connect with your children. With time, effort, and self-awareness, you can break the cycle of emotional wounds and provide your children with the love, care, and support that they need to thrive.

If your wounded inner child is in charge of your children, the main issue is that generational trauma will continue to exist. This can cause your own problems to be passed down to your children, ultimately injuring their innocent and gentle inner selves.

There are several indications that suggest you could be passing on an unhealthy inner child to your children.

- unwillingness to share or acknowledge emotional expression
- reacting to your children based on your moods
- poorly handling their tantrums
- failing to spend enough time with them
- not recognizing and praising their accomplishments
- frequently criticizing their actions
- lacking trust in their intentions
- showing no interest in their interests
- not knowing who their friends are
- avoiding difficult discussions
- discouraging both their failures and successes
- ignoring their negative emotions
- frequently engaging in conflicts with your child

If your wounded inner child is causing you problems, there's no need to continue suffering. Take the time to listen and show compassion towards your inner child to start the healing process. Use the effects of your wounded inner child to understand the importance of healing. Then, prepare to embark on a step-by-step healing process.

You must be the change you wish to see in the world. –Mahatma Gandhi

Looking at how your inner child's wounds influence and often ruin your life, relationships, finances, happiness, and child's future is enough to make you want to be the change you'll see in the world. So, let's discover how you'll apply ancient practices and Eastern healing techniques that blend into the modern world's inner child work.

A MOMENT OF REFLECTION

A grown up is a child with layers on.
— WOODY HARRELSON

Before we move on to unlocking your inner child's healing power, let's take a moment to reflect.

We have much work still to do, but by now, you should have a clearer idea of who your inner child is and how they affect your way of being in the world.

How does that feel? Are you beginning to sense a feeling of peace, the calming wave of self-acceptance beginning to wash over you?

For me, it was incredibly affirming to discover my inner child and the role she played in my adult life. It allowed me to make sense of so much of what I had experienced and the beliefs I held about myself. This discovery gives you incredible power – as we'll explore further in the book.

Before we proceed, however, I'd like to ask for your help in extending this sense of peace and the opportunity for healing to more people. And don't worry – it won't take more than a few minutes of your time. All I'd like to ask you to do is leave a review.

By leaving a review of this book on Amazon, not only will you share your thoughts and insights, but you'll also let others know that healing is possible. If you feel that you haven't gathered enough information from the book just yet, remember that you can leave your review after you finish reading the entire book.

Your review will serve as a guiding light for new readers, showing them the path to self-acceptance, personal growth, and healing.

Thank you so much for helping me spread the word. I'm excited about the difference we can make together.

5

UNLOCK YOUR INNER CHILD'S HEALING POWER—TRANSFORM YOUR HABITS AND REINFORCE BOUNDARIES TO ACHIEVE LASTING CHANGE!

P reparing goals to make changes is 10 times more likely to succeed rather than if you have no goals. Planning your healing process will ensure success beyond your wildest dreams. You can follow a step-by-step approach through the HEAL journey. The HEAL journey will prepare your expectations and show you how to use the coming steps and why they work. What does HEAL mean?

H—Harvest Your Inner Child's Needs

Everything you've discovered thus far is to harvest your inner child's needs. You'll have to consider how the inner child's wounds need to heal. It's a recommended idea to meditate on your inner child's needs. So, this part of the HEAL journey won't require a step of its own. Instead, you can use self-reflection meditation to prepare yourself for the coming steps.

What Is Self-Reflection Meditation?

We are often so caught up in our hopes, goals, and worries that we end up losing the ability to think quietly. Although there are instances when we need to be productive and motivated, there are also moments when it's necessary to connect with our inner selves and be mindful of what's going on right now in this moment. Self-reflection meditation helps us understand what we think and want. The more we think about our feelings, thoughts, values, and viewpoints, the better we can see them for what they actually are.

Benefits of Self-Reflection Meditation

Self-reflection meditation is a powerful tool that allows individuals to delve into their inner selves to explore their thoughts, emotions, and behaviors, and gain insight into their experiences. Here are five benefits of self-reflection meditation:

1. **Improved self-awareness:** Self-reflection meditation helps individuals become more aware of their thoughts, emotions, and behaviors. By taking time to reflect on these aspects of themselves, individuals can better understand their motivations, values, and beliefs. This increased self-awareness can lead to improved decision-making, as well as greater self-acceptance and self-esteem.

2. **Reduced stress and anxiety:** Practicing self-reflection meditation can help individuals reduce stress and anxiety by providing a space for them to release negative thoughts and emotions. Through meditation, individuals can learn to observe their thoughts and emotions without judgment, which can help reduce the impact of stressors on their mental and physical health.

3. **Increased focus and concentration:** By practicing self-reflection meditation, individuals can improve their ability to focus and concentrate. This is because meditation requires individuals to focus their attention on their breath or other objects, which can help develop greater concentration skills.

4. **Improved relationships:** Self-reflection meditation can help individuals become more mindful and present in their relationships. By becoming more aware of their thoughts and emotions, individuals can develop greater empathy and understanding towards others. This can lead to improved communication and deeper, more fulfilling relationships.

5. **Greater resilience:** By regularly practicing self-reflection meditation, individuals can develop greater resilience to life's challenges. By meditating, individuals can observe their emotions and thoughts without becoming overwhelmed by them. This can help individuals better cope with stressors and challenges and develop greater emotional stability and resilience.

Whole System Healing: The Start of Covering Everything You Discovered Up to This Point—Reflective Practices

Reflective practices help us become more aware of how we are feeling. Mindful, reflective thinking brings us back to ourselves and helps us get to know our bodies, emotions, thoughts, and spirits better. This gives us a chance to start over with a new sense of balance and harmony.

When people hear the words "reflective practice," they often think of sitting down and meditating. However, there are many other ways to reflect and think. For many people, prayer is a time for deep thought. Reflections includes walking meditation and other moving forms, such as yoga or Tai Chi. Journaling, making music, and making art are all reflective practices if they are done with the goal of focusing the mind.

We give tips on many different practices in this section of the book.

Our own physical, emotional, and spiritual roots are where

health starts. We can't really help heal other people or the world around us until we know what's happening with ourselves and take steps to get back into balance.

When we think about things and give them thought, we become more willing to see them as they are, not as we think they should be. We find that we can let go of the usual boundaries and hierarchies we set up for ourselves, as well as our many doubts, worries, plans, regrets, goals, and other thoughts that keep us from being present.

Like other people who practice whole system leadership, we stop being reactive and instead focus on deep listening. We let go of the need to control how things turn out and let many different ideas and points of view come up. We have faith that the group will come up with the right answer.

Meditate

Meditation is in no way a secret practice. Anyone can meditate. All we need is to make time during which we can avoid interruptions and a place where we can sit or lie down peacefully and bring our bodies to a state of stillness.

We can meditate for only a few minutes, or we can do it for a long time if we want to. Once we've stopped doing things, turned off our computers and phones, and calmed down, we can pay gentle, soft attention to the breath. And when sensations, sounds, feelings, emotions, and thoughts come up, which they always do, we just return, patiently and attentively, to the easy movement of the breath in the body. The following link provides an example of mindfulness meditation you can try out: https://www.youtube.com/watch?v=ZToicYcHIOU

Here Are Some Tips to Get You Going:

Try to meditate for 10–15 minutes a day to start. If you can, sit down at the same time every day, like when you wake up or at lunch.

Do your best to make this a regular habit because habits are a good way to build healthy lifestyles. If you haven't meditated by the time you go to bed, you can sit up in bed for 10 minutes, focus on your breath, and meditate before you go to sleep.

You don't have to sit on a meditation cushion to be reflective. You can be reflective at any time. Find a video that guides you through meditation to help you get started. If you need to take a quick break at work, you can find many 7 to 12 minute versions online.

Here is an example of a 10-minute self-reflection meditation exercise: https://www.youtube.com/watch?v=8BO9ylK9vFU

Awareness of the Present

Moment-to-moment awareness can be used in everyday life. Start by just being aware of what's going on in your body.

Do you feel open and loose right now, or do you feel heavy and tight? How are your lungs? Is your breathing in the chest or in the belly? Is it deep or shallow? Is it tight or loose? Taking note of your body can help you stay in the present moment and be aware of your feelings and thoughts.

Mindfulness and Deep Listening

Deep listening is one of the most important parts of healing whole systems. This is true for everything from gentle action to leadership to restorative dialogue. In addition to being aware of our own feelings, we can also work on really listening to others.

In mindful listening, we let go of what we think we know and how we felt in the past about a person or situation and just listen to what is being said. We don't try to change the other person's feelings and don't let our own feelings and opinions get in the way. Instead, we try to understand what they're going through.

Going for a Walk

Walk around your neighborhood slowly. Pay attention to seeing as you do. Don't try to figure out what it means or create an opinion about it. Instead, just look at the colors, light, and movement.

Then try to listen. Again, just listen to the sounds and don't try to figure out what's going on.

Then move on to how your body feels. As you walk, pay attention to how your body feels. When your feet touch the ground, how do they feel? How fast or slow are you going? Your arms are at your sides, right?

Give each of these three things 30–60 seconds of your attention and keep switching between them as you walk.

Journaling

Journaling is another way to practice mindfulness. This is when you write down how you feel as the emotions come and go. You could write down that you're worried, angry, or defensive, or that you are happy, sure of yourself, and satisfied.

Practice this in different situations so you can start to understand how you're feeling at any given time, and as a result, how you're responding to situations and people in your daily life. The point isn't to try to change how you feel, but to understand how your body and mind are right now by paying close attention to them.

By letting your hand and pen move across the page or your fingers fly across a keyboard, you can make it easier for your feelings, emotions, and thoughts to come out.

And now, with my *Inner Child Healing: Journaling Prompts* book, you have an incredible tool to guide you through this self-discovery journey. Use the prompts provided in this 314-page journal to dive deeper into your inner child's emotions and experiences. These prompts are designed to help you connect with your inner child, heal past wounds, and foster personal growth.

The key to journaling as a way to reflect is not to censor yourself or stop to try to gather and organize your thoughts. You're not editing, so stop being so hard on yourself. Just write. Don't hold back.

If you can't think of what to write next, keep your hand or

fingers moving by writing "I can't think of anything else" over and over again until your mind clears, and more words come.

Like meditation, this is something that is best done on a regular basis. Then it's easier for the mind and heart to open. But you can also write in a journal when you want to be alone, to help solve a problem, or to get closer to and feel more deeply about something.

ART AND MUSIC

Music and art can help us remember who we are. Choose a song you really like and sit down to listen to it. Do nothing but let it wash over you and envelop you. Afterward, note how you feel. *(If you want, you can show this to someone and see what happens.)* Do the same thing with a favorite piece of art. Simply sit and look at it. What do you like about it? Why? How do you feel now that you've looked at it?

Coloring

Coloring can serve as a potent tool for unlocking the healing potential of your inner child. My *Inner Child Healing: Coloring Book* offers a therapeutic and creative outlet for self-expression, enabling you to delve into your emotions and memories in a unique and profound way. Coloring engages both your mind and the sense of wonder within your inner child, facilitating a reconnection with long-forgotten feelings and experiences.

As you immerse yourself in the pages of this coloring book, you'll discover that the act of coloring can be incredibly soothing and meditative. It has the capacity to help you alleviate stress, anxiety, and the incessant chatter of your thoughts, mirroring the therapeutic benefits of musical improvisation. The rhythmic strokes of your colored pencils or markers can gently guide you back to the present moment, strengthening your connection with your inner child.

Furthermore, coloring nurtures a sense of control and creativity, which can be especially empowering if you are starting a journey of healing and self-discovery. By selecting colors, employing shading techniques, and experimenting with blending, you can symbolically take charge of your healing process, reinforce your boundaries, and gain a deeper understanding of your emotions and needs.

Improvisation

Improvisation, like in music and art, is another way to stop our thoughts from going in circles and come back to the present moment. To improvise, you have to be in the moment and pay attention to what is going on. If you want to improvise with a group, you have to let go of control and react to what other people do.

What Happens When We Reflect?

Reflective meditation is a good practice that helps people see clearly and precisely what their strengths and responsibilities are. So, when we reflect, we set aside time on purpose to think about what we've done, what's important to us now, and what we want to do in the future. If we want to do this reflection with intent and clearness, we need the peace of mind we get from practicing mindfulness regularly.

Reflecting on your inner child's needs will unravel every step of the HEAL journey, allowing you to reflect on the inner child's wounds. Pay special attention to how the wounds present in your body, where they present, and how they make you feel. See the inner child as a toddler waiting for some compassionate guidance, crying to make you hear what it has to say. Reach out to your inner child, paying close attention to the pains in your body, the sensations in your heart, and the thoughts in your mind during the session.

Precautions and Warnings Before You Engage in Self-Reflection Meditation Activities

Especially pay attention to any discomfort or sensations in

your solar plexus, which makes up a great part of your sympathetic nervous system, connected to your primal brain and inner child. There may be other health care problems that relate to this pain, which you will need to discuss with your health care practitioner.

What Exactly Is the Solar Plexus?

The solar plexus, also known as the celiac plexus, is a network of nerves and ganglia located in the abdominal area. It is an integral part of the sympathetic nervous system and is positioned in front of the aorta. This complex system is responsible for regulating the functioning of various organs, including the stomach, kidneys, liver, and adrenal glands. Solar plexus pain can result from various physical and emotional conditions.

The solar plexus is a critical component of the body's autonomic nervous system, which regulates bodily functions beyond conscious control. It is responsible for regulating digestion and metabolism, as well as controlling the fight-or-flight response to stress. The solar plexus can be influenced by emotions such as anxiety and fear, leading to sensations such as "butterflies in the stomach."

Solar plexus pain can be caused by factors, such as injury or inflammation of the surrounding tissues or organs. Emotional stress, anxiety, and trauma can also cause solar plexus pain, as the physical and emotional sensations are closely linked. Treatment for solar plexus pain may involve a combination of physical and psychological approaches, such as massage, relaxation techniques, and therapy.

The solar plexus is responsible for regulating many essential bodily functions. Understanding its role can help individuals take steps to maintain balance and alleviate pain or discomfort in this area.

E—Explore the Twin Flame Journey

This section is not for everyone. I was fortunate to connect with my twin flame, but not everyone goes through the twin flame journey and some people do not have a twin. For those who have discovered and undergone the twin flame journey during separation, this inner child healing section can help you and your twin come into union in the 5D, and eventually, the 3D physical world.

The twin flame journey is a spiritual and emotional experience that involves two individuals who are believed to share a single soul. The twin flame journey is a process of self-discovery and personal growth that occurs when two individuals reunite after being separated at a soul level (Tell, n.d.).

The twin flame journey involves a deep sense of connection and recognition between the two individuals, often accompanied by intense emotions and a sense of purpose. The journey is said to be marked by stages of separation and reunion, as the individuals work through their personal issues and come into alignment with their higher selves.

During the twin flame journey, both individuals may experience significant spiritual growth, as they confront their fears, heal past wounds, and learn to love unconditionally. While the journey can be challenging and emotionally intense, it is believed to lead to a deep sense of fulfillment and spiritual awakening for those who undertake it. Usually, one twin does the healing work first and their counterpart benefits from it. When they reunite after separation, they can continue to heal together because healing the inner child can help the twins reunite.

The twin flame journey is a deeply personal and transformative experience on the path to spiritual growth.

What Is the Conscious and Subconscious Start of the Twin Flame Journey?

The concept of the twin flame refers to the idea that there is a soul connection between two people that goes beyond the physical and emotional realm. The journey of the twin flame can be divided into two parts—the conscious start and the subconscious start.

The conscious start of the twin flame journey usually happens when two individuals meet and feel an instant and deep connection. This connection may manifest as a strong attraction, a feeling of familiarity, or an inexplicable pull towards each other. This initial meeting can be powerful and transformative and often leads to a period of intense attraction and infatuation.

However, the conscious start of the twin flame journey is just the tip of the iceberg. The real journey begins when the subconscious aspects of the connection come into play. This is when the deeper spiritual and emotional aspects of the twin flame connection start to emerge.

The subconscious start of the twin flame journey is often marked by a period of separation, conflict, or intense emotional turmoil. This is because the twin flame connection is meant to trigger deep healing and growth, and this process can be challenging and painful at times.

During the subconscious start of the twin flame journey, individuals may experience a range of emotions, including fear, anxiety, confusion, and intense longing. This is because the twin flame connection is meant to help individuals confront their deepest fears and insecurities.

The twin flame journey is a spiritual path that involves meeting and connecting with one's twin flame, a special soulmate that is said to share the same soul as oneself. The "twin flame" journey is often described as a transformative experience that can trigger deep healing and spiritual growth.

One important aspect of the twin flame journey is the healing of the inner child. As mentioned earlier, the inner child represents our childhood self and can carry the wounds and traumas from our past into our adult life. When they come together, their energies can trigger each other's inner child wounds, bringing them to the surface for healing.

Through the twin flame journey, individuals can work on healing their inner child wounds together, supporting each other in the process. This can involve identifying and acknowledging past traumas, offering comfort and validation to each other's inner child, and creating a safe and nurturing space for healing.

Healing the inner child on the twin flame journey can be a transformative experience that can lead to greater emotional and spiritual growth. As individuals heal their inner child wounds, they can become more grounded, balanced, and whole, allowing them to approach their twin flame connection from a place of emotional maturity and spiritual alignment.

By working together to identify and heal past wounds, individuals can create a strong foundation for a deeper and more meaningful connection with their twin flame. Through this healing process, individuals can also experience greater emotional and spiritual growth, leading to a more fulfilling and authentic life, but it requires a willingness to confront the darkest aspects of oneself to emerge into the light.

Conflicts That the Twin Flame Must Overcome and How They Can Achieve It

One of the primary sources of conflict for the twin flame is their individual and shared traumas, fears, and insecurities. The twin flame connection is meant to bring up these deep-seated issues, so they can be acknowledged, healed, and integrated through self-reflection, introspection, and healing work. This is a difficult process because it involves significant conflict and tension within the relationship.

Another important aspect of the twin flame journey is the concept of mirrored selves. Mirrored selves refer to the idea that they share a deep soul connection and mirror each other's strengths, weaknesses, and innermost desires. This mirroring can often manifest in the form of challenging experiences and conflicts within the twin flame relationship, as they sometimes won't like what they see.

When they meet, they often feel an intense soul recognition and a deep sense of familiarity with each other. This recognition is based on the shared soul energy that they possess and the mirroring of each other's energies. However, this mirroring can also bring up deep-seated issues and wounds that each twin flame may carry within themselves, making the twin flame journey a challenging and often tumultuous experience.

One way in which the mirroring effect can play out is through the differences that they may have in terms of personality, values, beliefs, and goals. These differences can create tension and conflict within the twin flame relationship, as each twin flame may struggle to understand and accept the other's perspective. However, through this conflict, they can also learn from each other and grow in ways that they may not have been able to do on their own.

To navigate the challenges of the twin flame journey, it is important for them to recognize and acknowledge the mirrored aspects of themselves and their relationship. By doing so, they can work together to heal and integrate their shared wounds and differences, leading to a deeper and more fulfilling connection.

To overcome the conflicts that arise on the twin flame journey, they must learn to communicate openly and honestly with each other. This means being willing to share their deepest fears and insecurities, as well as their hopes and dreams for the future. It also means being willing to listen to and empathize with their partner's perspective, even if it differs from their own.

They must also be willing to engage in healing work individually and together. This can involve practices such as therapy, meditation, energy work, and spiritual practices that can help them to confront and integrate their individual and shared traumas, fears, and insecurities.

They must be willing to cultivate a deep sense of trust and mutual respect within their relationship. This means being willing to forgive each other for mistakes and missteps and working together to find solutions to any conflicts that arise.

Ultimately, the key to overcoming conflict on the twin flame journey is to approach it with a willingness to learn, grow, and evolve. This means being open to feedback and constructive criticism, as well as being willing to acknowledge and work through their own shortcomings and limitations. By approaching conflict in this way, they can create a strong and harmonious connection that can serve as a foundation for spiritual growth and evolution.

How Does the Twin Flame Connection Help With Your Inner Child HEALing?

Because the inner child is the part of us that carries unresolved emotions and traumas from childhood, it can manifest in our adult lives as emotional wounds, limiting beliefs, and self-sabotaging behaviors. In the twin flame connection, the intense and deep connection can trigger these unresolved emotions and traumas to come to the surface, providing an opportunity for healing and integration. This can involve working through childhood wounds and patterns of behavior that no longer serve us, as well as learning to cultivate self-love, compassion, and inner strength.

By working through these issues within the twin flame connection, individuals can experience profound healing and transformation. They can learn to embrace their authentic selves, let go of past traumas, and cultivate a deep sense of self-love and acceptance. This can help them to heal their inner child wounds and move forward on their spiritual journey with greater clarity, purpose, and fulfillment.

Love seems to reconnect them, creating a union, stemming from ancient Eastern philosophy. So, how does this relate to your inner child healing? Self-love is a powerful tool to reconnect them, to bring karma and luck back into one soul, and to unite wholeness. So, your healing journey will require you to seek and practice a self-love routine to encourage and ignite the twin flame union.

A—Activate Your Boundaries

Boundaries can play a crucial role in healing your inner child in various ways. Here are some ways in which boundaries can help you build self-esteem, improve self-awareness, activate your self-love and self-improvement:

- **Builds self-esteem:** Setting boundaries for yourself can help you understand your self-worth and value. When you establish and enforce your limits, you're communicating to yourself that you're deserving of respect, care, and consideration. This can help you build self-esteem and confidence, as you're asserting yourself and prioritizing your needs.
- **Improves self-awareness:** When you set boundaries, you're forced to reflect on what's important to you and what you're willing to tolerate. This process can help you become more self-aware and gain a deeper understanding of your values, goals, and priorities. Additionally, by communicating your boundaries to others, you're also improving your communication skills and increasing your emotional intelligence.
- **Activates your self-love and self-improvement:** Boundaries can also activate your self-love and self-improvement by encouraging you to prioritize self-

care, personal growth, and self-improvement. By
saying "no" to things that don't align with your
values or goals, you're making space for things that
do and prioritizing your overall wellbeing. This can
help you develop a greater sense of self-love, as
you're taking care of yourself and valuing your
needs.

Setting and enforcing boundaries can be an empowering
way to heal your inner child and help yourself move towards a
healthier, more fulfilling life.

Boundaries can act as internal protection for your inner
child because they help create a safe and supportive environment that meets the child's emotional, psychological, and physical needs. Here's how boundaries can protect you:

- **Emotional protection:** Boundaries can protect the
  inner child's emotional wellbeing by setting limits
  on what they're willing to accept from others. By
  setting emotional boundaries, the inner child can
  protect themselves from emotional abuse,
  manipulation, and neglect. For instance, if someone
  constantly criticizes or belittles the inner child,
  setting a boundary of not tolerating such behavior
  can help protect their emotional state.
- **Psychological protection:** Boundaries can also
  protect the inner child's psychological wellbeing by
  establishing clear limits on what they're willing to
  tolerate in their relationships. By setting
  psychological boundaries, the inner child can
  protect themselves from being taken advantage of or
  manipulated by others. For instance, setting a
  boundary of not engaging in toxic conversations or

gossip can help protect the inner child's self-esteem and psychological wellbeing.

- **Physical protection**: Boundaries can also protect the inner child's physical wellbeing by setting limits on what they're willing to accept in their physical environment. By setting physical boundaries, the inner child can protect themselves from harm, danger, or abuse. For instance, setting a boundary of not tolerating physical abuse or violence can help protect the inner child's physical safety.

The situation I found myself in as a young child, being abandoned on the side of the road, is a perfect example of emotional abuse by a parent. However, if the emotional abuse carries on into adulthood; for example, the parent verbally abusing the child in front of their grandchildren or belittling them about how they look and act; the adult self should set boundaries to either stop the behavior or walk away from it. A person suffering emotional abuse may set boundaries with their parent or parents by choosing to limit their communication or interaction with them. By doing so, the person is protecting their emotional wellbeing and preventing further emotional harm. The person may also set psychological boundaries by not tolerating any manipulative behavior from their parent. By setting these boundaries, the person is creating a safe and supportive environment for their inner child to heal and grow.

Self-reflection on your inner child's specific needs and the act of self-love to unite the twin flame within your soul will help you understand what boundaries need to be in place to protect your inner child from further wounds while it heals.

Setting and enforcing boundaries can reinforce habit changes, form a healthy personal relationship with your inner child, and teach you to say no. Here's how:

- **Boundaries reinforce habit changes:** Boundaries can help reinforce habit changes by setting clear limits and expectations for yourself. When you set boundaries around a specific behavior or habit, you're creating a structure that supports your desire to change. For instance, if you're trying to quit smoking, setting a boundary of not smoking in your home or car can reinforce your commitment to change and help you avoid triggers that may lead to relapse.
- **It forms a healthy, personal relationship with your inner child:** Setting and enforcing boundaries can also help form a healthy personal relationship with your inner child. By listening to your inner child's needs and establishing clear boundaries that support their wellbeing, you're demonstrating self-love and compassion. This can help strengthen the bond between you and your inner child and foster a sense of trust and safety within yourself.
- **It teaches you to say no:** Setting and enforcing boundaries also teaches you to say no, which is a crucial skill for maintaining healthy relationships and achieving your goals. By setting clear limits and communicating your needs effectively, you're demonstrating self-respect and establishing healthy boundaries in your relationships. This can help you avoid burnout, reduce stress, and protect your wellbeing.

Discover how establishing healthier relations with your inner child can be the key to transforming your habits for good. By rewarding positive behavior loops and avoiding triggers that lead to negative habits, you can break free from self-sabotage and make lasting changes in your life.

Learn valuable techniques for setting and enforcing various types of boundaries that meet the needs of your inner child and habit loops. With this essential step in your healing journey, you'll gain the power to take control of your life and achieve lasting change. Don't miss out on this transformative opportunity! You're on the path to living a fulfilling and authentic life.

L—Lead Your New Habits Consciously

So, if your inner child is busy controlling your mind automatically, how can you pursue habit changes through your conscious mind?

Chakra Practices Introduce the Duality of Your Identity

The word *chakra* means disk or wheel (Lindberg, 2020). It refers to energy areas in the body that are thought to be important for physical, mental, and spiritual health.

Chakra techniques are a religious practice that started in old India and are now used in many types of complementary therapies and yoga. In chakra routines, most people focus on the seven primary chakras, which are each located at a different place along the spine.

The idea of division within the self constitutes one of the most important lessons that chakra routines convey. Each chakra is connected to a different part of the self, and by engaging with these energy areas, people can learn more about themselves and find a balance between their different parts. For example, the root chakra, which is at the base of the spine, is related to the human body and survival mechanisms, while the crown chakra, which is at the top of the head, is related to spiritual connection and greater awareness.

By working with their chakras, people can learn more about the different parts of themselves and how they fit together. People can bring harmony and equilibrium to their chakras and feel more whole within themselves by doing things like meditation, visualizing, and doing yoga moves.

Chakra routines can be a strong way to learn about how the mind and body are connected and improve your health as a whole. By showing the multifaceted nature of the self, chakra practices urge people to discover and accept all parts of who they are. This leads to more self-awareness, balance, and peace of mind.

Do You Know Your Seven Primary Chakras?

There are seven key chakras located along your spine, each in a different location (Heyl, 2023):

- **Crown:** Your crown chakra, also known as *Sahasrara*, is situated on top of your head. It's your spiritual link to yourself, everyone else, and the universe. It also has an impact on your life's mission.
- **Third Eye:** *Ajna*, also known as the third eye chakra, is situated between your eyebrows. This chakra is responsible for your strong gut instinct because the third eye is in charge of intuition. It is also associated with imagination.
- **Throat:** *Vishuddha*, or throat chakra, is positioned in your throat. This chakra governs our confidence to communicate verbally.
- **Heart:** This chakra, also known as *Anahata*, is situated in the middle of your chest, near your heart. It is concerned with our capacity for love and compassion.
- **Solar Plexus:** This chakra, also known as *Manipura*, is situated in your stomach. It is in charge of your confidence, self-esteem, and the capability to feel in control of your life and circumstances.
- **Sacral:** *Svadhisthana*, or the sacral chakra, is positioned underneath your belly button. This

chakra governs your artistic and sexual energy. It is also connected to how you connect to your own and other people's emotions.

- **Root**: *Muladhara*, or the root chakra, is placed at the bottom of your spine. It gives you a foundation for life and helps you to feel grounded and competent in overcoming challenges. The root chakra is in charge of your feeling of safety and stability.

How Does an Unbalanced Chakra Affect Your Wellbeing?

Energy flow depletion or excessive energized activity in a chakra can result in different outcomes. When a chakra lacks energy, it is difficult to express the values connected to that chakra. When a chakra is overactive, the qualities it represents become a ruling force in a human being's life. It can have physical and psychological consequences. Take the first chakra about security, survival, and the foundation of our life as an example. When it is inactive, it can manifest in your life as depression and insecurity. When there is an excess of energy, it can manifest as courage without precaution or over eagerness to hoard material possessions because you require more to feel secure.

Integrating Chakra Healing and Meditation Into Your Journey

Your body shows what you think about, what you feel, and experience in your heart and mind. Every thought and feeling you've ever had is written down in your body. Your tissue cells, fluids, and organ functioning do just as much processing of your thoughts, feelings, and surroundings as your mind does. The same is true for your spirit. Your spirit is linked to what you feel in your body and what you think in your thoughts.

The chakra concept assists in helping you understand that you are not a jigsaw puzzle with merely three pieces that make up your spirit, body, and mind. Instead, you are a uniquely created person. Yes, there is synergy and communication between your mind and body.

Chakra healing and meditation are a pivotal point of integration for the journey. Chakra meditation integrates a conscious perspective of your mind, body, and inner child. Chakra healing allows you to pinpoint the exact blockages in your energy, welcoming the twin flame restoration.

How Can Chakra Healing Change How Your Inner Child Responds in the Future?

If you don't deal with the people and things that have affected your inner child in the past and the things that happen to you in your present life, they can have a huge effect on your mental and physical wellbeing. Chakra energy can get stuck or stopped, which can make your body feel out of balance. For example, if you can't deal with the loss of a loved one, it can show up as lung problems. Or if you were bullied as a child, the energy can stay in your nervous system, and you might carry it into future relationships.

On the other hand, you won't carry your mental issues into the future if you deal with your past through chakra repair. Your past won't have as much influence over you, and you'll be less likely to do things that hurt yourself.

Steps of Chakra Healing

Chakra healing involves many steps, which may vary depending on the specific approach used. Common steps to help you with chakra healing include (Shah, 2020; Monroe, n.d.):

- **Diagnosis:** In Chapter 8, we discuss the signs of a blocked chakra. This may help you identify your symptoms.
- **Clearing:** As soon as you have identified a blockage, you may use the techniques discussed in Chapter 8 to clear your chakra and restore the balance. This

may involve energy healing techniques such as meditation, Reiki, visualization, and even music.

- **Balancing:** After the chakra has been cleared, you may work to balance the energy flow in the chakra. This may involve using stones or crystals, aromatherapy, or other tools to support the chakra's energy flow.
- **Integration:** The final step of chakra healing involves integrating the changes made during the healing process into your daily routine including self-care practices, such as meditation, yoga, or lifestyle changes that can support ongoing chakra health.

Chakra healing is a complementary therapy and should not replace medical treatment for serious health conditions. Please make sure that you consult with your healthcare practitioner first in case of serious conditions.

Healing takes courage, and we all have courage, even if we have to dig a little to find it. –Tori Amos

Courage will go a long way to ensure your step-by-step inner child healing works and lasts. Congratulate yourself if you've come this far, you have already gained some courage! In Chapter 8, we'll talk specifically about healing the different chakras. Now, let's put your courage to work with the act of loving yourself.

6

EXPLORE THE TWIN FLAME JOURNEY FOR INNER CHILD HEALING

About 44% of people think of self-care as an activity for those with time, and 35% think of it as an activity for people with money (Cassata, 2019). Yet, surprisingly, we wonder why inner child work is gaining popularity.

Ignoring the self, the constant voice of your inner child, and suppressing your subconscious feelings won't help your healing process. You require love, compassion, respect, and care, so does your inner child. So, let's get right to it.

Do you think it is possible to love yourself? Stop doubting yourself right now and engage on the twin flame journey with love, compassion, and a deep understanding of what your inner child needs. Start your steps as soon as you practice self-reflection meditation, opening your mind to how much you need self-love, self-care, self-compassion, and self-respect. It's time to start with the reparenting of your inner child to heal the twin flame that brings wholeness to your life, relationships, and everything about you.

Use Reparenting to Unite Your Twin Flame Connection

Reparenting Through Self-Care
There are different types of self-care that you need to apply:

- **Physical:** Sleeping seven to eight hours a night; taking a walk during lunch breaks; staying hydrated; going to the gym; etc.
- **Emotional:** Activities that allow you to connect, deal with, and think about all of your feelings. For example, talking to a counselor; keeping a diary; drawing, painting, or other art; playing music; dancing; etc.
- **Practical:** You do tasks that are important to your life, so you can prevent difficult situations in the future. For example, taking classes to improve your career; compiling a budget; cleaning out your closet; writing out a daily planning schedule; eating when you need to; preparing meals for the week in advance; etc.
- **Mental:** Any exercise that stimulates your thinking processes or makes you wiser.
- **Social:** Activities that help you care for and get to know the people in your life better. Having breakfast with friends; going on a date if you're in need of companionship; a mom's night out; making time to phone your parents regularly; etc.
- **Spiritual:** Activities that make you feel good and help you think about things more significant than yourself. Self-care on a spiritual level doesn't have to be religious, but for some people, it is. For example, meditation; yoga; visiting a place of worship; spending time in nature; giving yourself time to think; helping out at a shelter; etc.

Reparenting Through Self-Love
To practice self-love and heal your inner child through the twin flame union, you can:

- Change your conscious dialogue—talk positively to and about yourself.
- Put your needs first and set boundaries.
- Believe in yourself and be truthful.
- Listen to your body and your inner child, be kind to yourself, forgive yourself, and accept yourself.
- When you need to, take a break.
- Prioritize needs over desires.
- Try meditating, accept yourself, not judging, and loving kindness.

Reparenting Through Self-Compassion
Uniting the twin flame with self-compassion toward your inner child means bringing together the masculine and feminine parts of yourself, which is what the twin flame concept is all about. It means developing a deep sense of compassion and understanding for your inner child, which is the part of you that is hurt, vulnerable, and emotional and may have been neglected in the past. By being kind to your inner child, you can start to heal these wounds and bring all of your parts together to make you a more balanced and whole person, which can help your relationships with other people and your overall sense of wellbeing.

Using compassion meditation is the ultimate practice to show your inner child how much you care to unite the twin flame.

Seeing yourself suffer is painful. Learn to practice self-soothing and compassion towards your inner child.

How to Do This Practice:

- Find a quiet place, sit down, and make yourself at home. When you're ready, close your eyes slowly.
- Relax your body by taking deep breaths. Let go of stress in different parts of your body, one at a time.
- Think of a hard time you went through. Keep a mental picture of that time for yourself.
- Reflect on whatever it is you are or were struggling with. Mentally, make some wishes of compassion for yourself. For example, "May my inner child be free from pain."

List some positive affirmations that you can say out aloud to yourself when you are alone. Use these positive affirmations as part of your meditation exercises. For example:

- I am strong, brave, and kind.
- I have given it my best shot.
- I know I can do this.
- I'm a beautiful, unique person.
- I am fearless.
- I am a good friend.
- My dreams are possible.

Reparenting Through Self-Respect

Self-respect means that you care for yourself and love yourself. It happens when you adhere to your values and aren't willing to give in. Being your authentic self in life. The more you act in ways that match your values and principles, the happier and surer of yourself you'll feel. In turn, this will make you feel better about yourself. When you respect yourself, you don't compare yourself or your life to other people's. In today's digital and competitive world, this may be even more important.

What Does Self-Respect Consist Of?

- Pay attention to what you like.
- Think about what you believe and why you believe it.
- Take stock of the relationships you don't need, those that no longer serve you, and get rid of them.
- Take care of the needs of your inner child.

That's it, loving, respecting, and honoring your inner child are the most effective ways to reparent it for a twin flame union, setting the foundation for what comes next. These practices must become part of your daily life to have lasting effects and reward your inner child for changing the coming habits.

Love yourself first, and everything else falls in line. –Lucille Ball

Your healing begins as soon as you learn to love yourself, ultimately setting a stage for changes in your inner child's habits and removing past wounds. Honor your inner child enough to reparent it as though it were a toddler. Then, it's time to set boundaries to protect the toddler and goals to feed its needs.

7

ACTIVATE YOUR BOUNDARIES TO PROTECT THE PRECIOUS INNER CHILD

Let us listen to the needs of our inner child that is being tamed and imprisoned by the rules of a grown-up world. –Erik Pevernagie

You're four times more likely to be successful if you write your goals and boundaries down. However, you won't find much success in healing your inner child or reparenting your habits and thoughts if you don't know how goals and boundaries work. Boundaries aren't simply an idea to heal the inner child. They're set to protect what you're starting to love, and they'll set everything in motion for the final step: integration. Let's discover the secrets to setting goals and boundaries for unbreakable and unshakeable results.

Do you remember how you used self-reflection to become more aware of everything that went wrong in your life? Do you remember how you discovered the common signs of a wounded inner child? Well, it's time to choose the changes you want to make and set them in stone.

Before setting realistic boundaries, design a set of goals or outcomes you'd like to achieve in changing your inner child's trauma. Outcomes mean everything, and they'll guide your boundaries to keep them realistic and committed. Let's discover how unbreakable goals look. Keep your pen and paper close for this one.

What Benefits Come From Setting Realistic Goals and Boundaries?

Setting goals and boundaries that are realistic can help you in both your personal and professional life in a number of ways. Some of them are:

- **Increased motivation:** When you set goals that are achievable but still challenging, you are more likely to feel motivated to work towards them. Unrealistic goals can be demotivating, as you may feel like you can never succeed no matter how hard you try.
- **Improved self-esteem:** Achieving goals can boost your self-esteem and give you a sense of accomplishment. When you set realistic goals and boundaries, you are more likely to achieve them, which can make you feel good about yourself and your abilities.
- **Better time-management:** Setting boundaries can help you manage your time effectively. By setting limits on when and how much you work, you can avoid burnout and ensure that you have time for other important activities, such as spending time with family and friends.
- **Reduced stress:** Setting boundaries can help reduce your stress. When you have clear boundaries, you are less likely to feel overwhelmed or overworked,

which can contribute to feelings of anxiety and stress.

- **Improved relationships**: Setting boundaries can help improve your relationships with others. By communicating your needs and expectations, you can avoid misunderstandings and conflicts and build stronger, more positive relationships.

Setting realistic goals and boundaries can help you achieve more, feel better about yourself, and improve your relationships and overall wellbeing.

How Do You Begin Choosing New Goals and Boundaries?

I used to struggle with setting boundaries due to my fear of abandonment that stemmed from my childhood. Growing up, I learned that women in my culture should always comply and not resist what is expected of them.

In both my personal and professional life, I would take on projects and responsibilities that were not mine, and I would not speak up about my own needs and wants. This led to feelings of resentment and anger, which eventually caused the demise of my marriage as I self-sabotaged the relationship.

It wasn't until I engaged in deep introspection and self-reflection that I realized I had been allowing others to intrude upon me physically, mentally, emotionally, and psychologically. I was overcommitting and sacrificing my own wellbeing to help others achieve their goals. I was the one responsible for my own misery and burnout. This may sound familiar to you too. How would you begin choosing new goals and boundaries?

It Begins With Being Aware of Yourself

Know that you can change the way you feel or act if you don't like it. You are in charge of everything that happens to you and to everyone else around you. Accept that you will be uncomfortable at first. It all starts with saying "no" to things that don't help you and standing up for yourself without feeling guilty or ashamed.

"No" Is a Valid Statement

It's not something you only do at specific times; it's a habit you have to keep up for the rest of your life if you want to reach your work and life objectives. What will be the first step you take towards contentment, fulfillment, and tranquility when it comes to setting healthy boundaries?

Draw the Line

I had to draw that invisible line in the sand to take action to protect myself, my plans, and my hopes for the future. Initially, I felt bad about letting other people down and didn't want to hurt anyone's feelings. But then I just started saying "no" without any other reasons or explanations. No turned into a complete sentence for me. Even though it surprised a few people, I stuck to my belief that I needed to set limits in my life.

SMART Goal Setting

To start the process of goal setting and achieving success, begin with a self-reflection meditation journey to identify any traumas haunting your inner child. Afterward, use a goal setting meditation to envision the outcomes you want to achieve and feel the sensations of your inner child as you do so.

Once you have a clear idea of your goals, write them down and place them where you can see them daily. However, ensure that your goals follow the SMART system for careful goal setting, which includes Specific, Measurable, Achievable, Relevant, and Time-based criteria.

Now that you know what changes your inner child needs for protection, healing, and improved automated responses, it's time to set boundaries related to your goals. For example, you might decline a coffee invitation with friends if you have an important work meeting that aligns with your goals, or you might refuse to allow your partner to mistreat you because your boundary doesn't permit anyone to abuse your inner child. Watch the following guided meditations on YouTube to assist with setting goals and boundaries in your life:

- https://www.youtube.com/watch?v=olmV_appq9I
- https://www.youtube.com/watch?v=HCZXr4UNCk8

Setting Your Boundaries for Nine Types of Inner Child Healing

You'll find nine types of boundaries, and yes, you need them all, even if you choose one boundary for each type at first. So, let's see examples of the types of boundaries and get some ideas on how to set them.

Emotional Boundaries

Emotional boundaries refer to the limits that individuals set for themselves in terms of their emotions, feelings, and behaviors in relationships with others. Setting healthy emotional boundaries is crucial for maintaining one's self-respect, self-esteem, and overall wellbeing.

Some examples of healthy emotional boundaries in relationships are being clear about your needs and communicating them well, saying "no" when you need to, respecting other people's feelings and needs, not putting up with emotional abuse or manipulation, and taking responsibility for your own emotional health.

Other examples of healthy emotional boundaries are not putting up with rude or hurtful behavior, taking time for yourself when you need it, and not letting other people decide how much you are worth.

Also, it is important to respect the boundaries of other people, even if they are different from your own.

People can set emotional boundaries by first figuring out how they feel, what they need, and what they value. This means being honest with yourself and recognizing when your values or needs are not being met through certain actions or situations.

It's important to say what your limits are in a clear, assertive way, using "I" statements, and avoiding language that blames or attacks. It's important to stick to one's boundaries by making sure there are consequences when they are broken.

Physical Boundaries

Physical boundaries are the limits that individuals set for themselves in terms of their personal space, touch, and physical contact with other people. Setting and maintaining healthy physical boundaries is crucial for maintaining one's sense of safety and personal autonomy in relationships.

Examples of healthy physical boundaries include not tolerating physical violence or abuse, saying "no" to unwanted physical contact, respecting other people's personal space and physical boundaries, and taking care of one's own physical health and wellbeing.

Other examples of healthy physical boundaries include not engaging in sexual activities before being ready, avoiding situations or activities that make one uncomfortable or unsafe, and setting limits on physical contact with certain individuals.

To set physical boundaries, individuals can start by identifying their own needs and comfort levels in terms of physical contact and personal space. It is also important to communicate one's physical boundaries clearly and assertively, using non-threatening words and body language.

It's important to enforce one's physical boundaries by setting consequences and following through when they are crossed. This may include ending a relationship or limiting contact with certain individuals who do not respect your physical boundaries.

Sexual Boundaries

Sexual boundaries are limits that we establish in our intimate relationships to ensure our physical, emotional, and mental safety and wellbeing. These boundaries vary from person to person and depend on our personal beliefs, values, and preferences. Here are some examples of sexual boundaries:

- **No means no**: This is an important rule that everyone should follow. No one should ever do anything sexual with anyone else without their permission.
- **Timing**: Different people may have different ideas about when they want to be sexual with their partners. It's important to talk to your partner about what your limits are and make sure you're both on the same page.
- **Sexual activities**: People may have different ideas about when and what type of sexual activities they want with their partners. It's important to let your partner know what your limits are and make sure you're both on the same page.
- **Privacy**: People have the right to privacy while engaging in sexual acts. It's important to set limits on how much you tell people about your intimate sexual life, as a result of self-respect and respect for your partner.
- **Protection**: To safeguard yourself and your partner from sexually transmitted infections (STIs), diseases, and unplanned pregnancies, you must use protection when you are sexually active.

Setting sexual limits can be hard, but it's important for your health and pleasure in relationships. Here are some suggestions for setting sexual limits:

- **Identify your values:** Take some time to think about what you believe and what you value when it comes to sex and intimacy. This will help you set limits that are in line with what you feel is right for you.
- **Communicate your boundaries:** It is important to communicate your boundaries clearly and assertively with your partner. Let them know what you are and are not comfortable with.
- **Be consistent:** Consistency is essential in establishing and maintaining boundaries. Stick to your boundaries and enforce them consistently.
- **Be willing to compromise:** While it is important to stick to your boundaries, be willing to compromise and find a middle ground that works for both you and your partner.
- **Trust your instincts:** If something feels uncomfortable or wrong, trust your instincts and speak up. Your feelings and intuition are valid, and it is important to prioritize your safety and wellbeing.

Workplace Boundaries

Workplace boundaries are the limits that people set for themselves at work to protect their physical, mental, and emotional health. Here are some examples of workplace boundaries:

- **Workload:** People have the right to set limits on their work and make sure they don't take on too much work that hurts their health and ability to get things done.
- **Off time:** People have the right to take time off of work for things like illness, family emergencies, and mental health days.

- **Communication:** People can set limits on how they talk to each other, like limiting emails or phone calls after work hours, to avoid burnout and keep a healthy work-life balance.
- **Personal space:** People can set limits on their own space and privacy, like not letting coworkers into their workspace without permission.
- **Physical contact:** People have the right to set limits on physical contact and make sure it's appropriate for work.

Setting boundaries at work can be hard, but it's important for your health and growth as a professional. Here are some tips to set workplace boundaries:

- **Identify your values:** Start taking time to reflect on your personal beliefs and values pertaining to work and professional relationships. This will help you set limits that are in line with what you value.
- **Tell people what your limits are:** It's important to tell your coworkers and bosses what your limits are in a clear and assertive way. Tell them what you're okay with and what you're not.
- **Be consistent:** Being consistent is important for setting and keeping boundaries. Stick to your rules and follow them every time.
- **Be willing to compromise:** It's important to stick to your own rules, but you should also be willing to find a middle ground that works for you and your coworkers.
- **Get help:** If you find it hard to set or keep boundaries, ask a trusted coworker, supervisor, or mentor for help.

Material Boundaries

Material boundaries are the limits that people put on their physical surroundings to protect their things and space. You can set limits on who can have access to your things, your personal space, and your money as part of these boundaries. Here are some examples of material boundaries:

- **Personal items**: People can set limits on their personal items by choosing who can use them and how often they can be borrowed or shared.
- **People have the right to set limits on their personal space and privacy.** For example, they can say that no one can come into their home or place of work without permission.
- **Financial resources**: People can set limits on their financial resources, like how much they can lend or borrow from others.
- **Time and energy**: People can set limits on their time and energy by saying "no" to requests or commitments that don't fit with their values or priorities.

Placing boundaries on money can be hard, but it's important for your health and happiness. Here are some tips to set material boundaries:

- **Identify your values**: Take some time to think about what you believe and what you value, when it comes to things and space. This will help you set limits that are in line with what you feel is right.
- **Communicate your boundaries**: It's important to be clear and firm about your limits with other people. Let them know what you are and are not comfortable with.

- **Be consistent:** When setting and keeping boundaries, it's important to be consistent. Stick to your rules and follow them every time.
- **Seek support:** If you find it hard to set or keep limits, talk to a trusted friend, family member, or therapist for help.
- **Practice self-care:** Setting limits can be hard and may cause you to feel guilty or anxious. It's important to take care of yourself and put your health first while setting limits.

Time Boundaries

People set limits on their time and commitments to protect their mental, emotional, and physical health. These limits are called *time boundaries*. Some of these limits can be set around work hours, social obligations, and time for self-care and relaxation. Here are some examples of time boundaries:

- **Work hours:** People can set limits on their work hours by giving themselves clear start and end times, limiting their overtime, and not bringing work home.
- **Social commitments:** Attending family gatherings, having dinner with friends, or pitching up at your social clubs after hours all place additional stress on your time for self-care and relaxation. You need to be able to say no and communicate your boundaries clearly.
- **Personal time:** People can set limits on their own time, so they can take care of themselves and relax. For example, they can schedule time for exercise, meditation, or hobbies.

- **Technology use:** People can set limits on how they use technology, such as how much time they spend on their screens.

Putting limits on your time can be hard, but it's important for your health and productivity. Here are some tips to set time boundaries:

- **Identify your priorities:** Take the time to figure out your time and commitment priorities and values. This will help you set limits that match your goals and values.
- **Communicate your boundaries:** It's important to be clear and firm about your limits with other people. Tell them what you're okay with and what you're not.
- **Be consistent:** When setting and keeping boundaries, it's important to be consistent. Stick to your time rules.
- **Say no:** Learn to say "no" to commitments or requests that do not align with your priorities or values.
- **Practice self-care:** Setting limits can be hard and may make you feel guilty or anxious. It's important to take care of yourself and put your health first while setting limits.

Intellectual Boundaries

Intellectual boundaries are the limits that people put on their thoughts, beliefs, and opinions to protect their intellectual health and help them communicate with others in a healthy way. Some of these boundaries are setting limits on discussions about sensitive topics, respecting the opinions of others, and not bullying or gaslighting people intellectually. Here are some examples of intellectual boundaries:

- **Sensitive topics**: People can set limits on sensitive topics, like politics, religion, and personal beliefs, by talking less about them or not talking about them at all.
- **Respect for others' opinions**: People can set limits by listening to and respecting the opinions of others, even if they don't agree with them.
- **Intellectual bullying**: People can set boundaries by not doing things like making fun of other people's ideas or thoughts or ignoring what they are thinking and feeling.
- **Gaslighting**: People can set boundaries by not gaslighting, which is when someone tricks someone else into doubting their own thoughts, feelings, or perceptions.

Setting intellectual boundaries can be hard, especially when people have different ideas or points of view. Here are some tips to set intellectual boundaries:

- **Clarify your own beliefs**: Take the time to figure out what you think and believe about sensitive topics. This will help you set clear limits on how you talk about these things.
- **Communicate your boundaries**: It's important to be clear and firm about your limits with other people. Tell them what you are and are not willing to talk about.
- **Respect others' opinions**: While it's important to set limits around sensitive topics, it's also important

to respect other people's opinions, even if you don't agree with them.

- **Set limits:** If someone is pushing your intellectual boundaries, you can set limits or leave the conversation.
- **Seek support:** If you find it hard to set or keep boundaries, ask a trusted friend or family member for help.

Financial Boundaries

The term *"financial boundaries"* refers to the limits that one places on their money to protect their financial health and encourage good money habits. These boundaries can include setting limits on spending, making clear expectations about who is responsible for what financially in a relationship, and staying away from financial codependence or enabling. Here are some examples of financial boundaries:

- **Spending limits:** People can limit their spending by making a budget, not buying things on impulse, and not spending money on things they don't need.
- **Clear expectations in relationships:** People can set limits on their financial responsibilities in romantic or family relationships by talking about and agreeing on things like bills, rent/mortgage, and household costs.
- **Financial enabling:** People can set limits on giving money to people who have a history of mismanaging their money or struggling with addiction by not giving anything to them.
- **Codependency:** People can set limits on codependency when it comes to money by not allowing others to use money to control or

manipulate them and by not self-controlling or manipulating others with money.

Setting financial limits can be hard, especially if you have to depend on money or are under financial pressure. Here are some tips to set financial boundaries:

- **Establish financial goals:** Take the time to set clear goals and priorities for your money. This will help you set limits that make sense for your financial goals.
- **Communicate your boundaries:** It's important to tell people clearly and firmly what your financial limits are. Tell them what you're okay with and what you're not.
- **Stick to your budget:** When setting and keeping financial limits, it's important to be consistent.
- **Avoid enabling behaviors:** It's important not to do things like give money to people who have a history of mismanaging money or being addicted to drugs.
- **Seek support:** If you find it hard to set or keep boundaries, talk to a financial advisor or therapist for help.

Non-Negotiable, Personal Boundaries

Non-negotiable personal boundaries are limits that individuals set to protect their physical, emotional, and mental wellbeing. These boundaries are non-negotiable, meaning that they cannot be compromised or altered. Non-negotiable boundaries are essential conditions that individuals require to feel secure, and they usually involve safety issues such as physical violence, emotional abuse, drug or alcohol use, fidelity, and life-threatening health problems. Here are some examples of non-negotiable personal boundaries: The installation of a pool fence before allowing children to visit, ending a relationship due to infidelity, or any other non-negotiable conditions that must be met to feel secure.

However, it is important to avoid having too many non-negotiable boundaries, as they lose their meaning if not enforced. It is necessary to follow through on non-negotiable boundaries; otherwise, they become counterproductive.

Having learned about the nine types of boundaries, it is my hope that you have gained a better understanding of the boundaries that are necessary for you. It is advisable to list them down as a means of holding yourself accountable for creating boundaries that will safeguard your wellbeing, establish or maintain your uniqueness, and allow you to focus your time, energy, and resources on things that are important to you.

How Will You Inform People About Your Boundaries?

It's important to be clear and direct about your limits if you want to get your point across. You should be clear and honest about how you feel or what you need. Even though it may be hard to set limits, it's important to accept the discomfort and push through it to make sure your needs are met. This may take time and effort, but it is an important part of taking care of yourself and keeping healthy boundaries in your relationships.

Build and Reserve Your Boundaries in Small Steps

Building and reserving your boundaries in small steps is a helpful approach to creating strong and healthy boundaries. It involves starting with small boundaries and gradually increasing them as you become more comfortable with the process. This approach can help you avoid feeling overwhelmed or stressed while also allowing you to build your confidence and assertiveness over time.

- Start early to set boundaries in your relationships, projects, job, and finances.
- Self-reflect on them often.
- Set small boundaries and grow them.
- Remain consistent.
- Use framework.
- Add extras or remove as you notice they need changing for your inner child.

If someone oversteps the line of your boundaries, don't change your inner child's narrative back to negative talk. Respond respectfully and reassert your boundaries again. Give the person a gentle and respectful warning but consider cutting your losses if they overstep the line again. Just be careful not to catastrophize the boundary break.

Be Wise, Don't Catastrophize

Catastrophizing is a cognitive distortion that involves magnifying or exaggerating the potential negative outcomes of a situation and imagining the worst possible scenarios. People who engage in catastrophizing may assume that small problems will escalate into major catastrophes, or they may expect the worst possible outcome in any given situation.

Catastrophizing is a common thought pattern associated with anxiety disorders, but it can also occur in people with depression or other mental health conditions. It can lead to increased anxiety, fear, and avoidance behaviors, which can negatively impact a person's quality of life.

Examples of catastrophizing include:

- Thinking that a small mistake at work will get you fired or keep you from getting another job ever again.

- Thinking that if you get turned down once in a relationship, you'll never find love or be happy again.
- Imagining the worst possible result of a medical test or procedure, like thinking a harmless lump is cancer before you have the diagnosis.

It can be hard to deal with catastrophizing on your own, but cognitive-behavioral therapy (CBT) can help. CBT helps people recognize and change negative thought patterns, like catastrophizing, with more positive and realistic ones. Practicing mindfulness and relaxation techniques, such as deep breathing and meditation, can also help reduce anxiety and manage catastrophizing.

Reflect on your behavior at all times. Has the other person really overstepped your boundaries, or is your response based on your wounded inner child's fears? If they have, it's time for you to say goodbye to bad relationships that wound your inner child even more. CBT highlights the importance of being self-aware and mindful of our responses to others.

When we react to a situation or person, it's essential to take a step back and examine whether our response is coming from a place of past traumas or hurts that our inner child is trying to protect us from. In some cases, our reactions may be influenced by past experiences, and it may not be an accurate representation of the current situation.

However, if after reflecting, we realize that the person did in fact cross a line or engage in behavior that is harmful or toxic, it's essential to take action and say goodbye to the bad relationship. This may involve setting boundaries, having difficult conversations, or even ending the relationship altogether.

By prioritizing the wellbeing of our inner child, we can make choices that are in alignment with our values and needs, rather than staying in relationships that wound us. This can be challenging, but it's essential for our emotional and mental health. Saying goodbye to bad relationships allows us to create space for healthy and supportive relationships that nourish and uplift our inner child.

By now, you hopefully already know what you want to change, which boundaries will encourage the change, and how you need to heal your inner child, how to reparent your subconscious mind, and rekindle your twin flame union.

Now, it's time to integrate the energy work that brings everything together.

8

LEAD YOUR NEW HABITS TO HEAL THE INNER CHILD'S WOUNDS

Energy is our first true language. The soul speaks this native tongue in every moment of every day. For it is a candid communication that cannot be concealed or silenced. –Anthony St. Martin

You've reflected, discovered, loved yourself, and handed the inner child an olive branch. Now, it's time to help the inner child heal, put the changes into action, and integrate the healing process for completely optimal results through chakra healing practices.

How to Use the Seven Chakras to Heal Your Inner Child

In Chapter 5, we learned that chakra techniques are a type of religious practice that started in old India and are now used in many types of complementary therapies and yoga. In chakra routines, most people focus on the seven primary chakras, which are each located at a different place along the spine. The idea of division within the self constitutes one of the most important lessons that chakra routines convey. Each chakra is connected to a different part of the self, and by engaging with these energy areas, people can learn more about themselves and find a balance between their different parts. People can bring harmony and equilibrium to their chakras and heal themselves by doing things like meditation, visualization, and yoga moves.

The chakras are energy centers located along the spine that correspond to different aspects of the physical, emotional, and spiritual self. Each chakra is associated with a specific color, element, set of crystals, recommended yoga poses, blockage signs, and controls different parts of the body and mind.

Root: Your First Chakra

The root chakra, also known as the *Muladhara* chakra, is located at the base of the spine, and is associated with the color red. Its element is earth, and the recommended crystals include red jasper and hematite. Recommended yoga poses for the root chakra include seated forward bend and mountain pose. It develops between the ages of one and seven and matches our core needs. Blockage signs can include feelings of insecurity, anxiety, and lack of stability. The root chakra controls your lower body, legs, feet and is associated with your sense of stability, safety, and survival. You can't do well if your root chakra is out of balance, just like a tree can never grow without a strong base. If this chakra is blocked or out of balance, it's likely that all of your other chakras, from the sacral to the crown, are too.

Signs of Root Chakra Blockage or Imbalance

- controlling actions
- anger quickly
- lack of will or drive
- feel awkward and insecure when you're around other people

- always tired or sluggish

How to Unblock Your Root Chakra

- **Envision the color red:** Start by meditating and visualizing a bright red light at the base of your tailbone, extending down your legs and feet, and into the ground to balance your root chakra.
- **Dance:** Dancing is an excellent way to become more comfortable in your body and balance your chakra. Singing along with music can also cleanse your throat chakra.
- **Practice tree pose:** Yoga postures like tree pose can cleanse the root chakra. Plant your left foot firmly, bring your right foot up, and be creative by engaging your core, reaching your arms overhead, and feeling connected to the earth.
- **Take a mindful shower:** Be present and embrace your physicality while bathing. Mindfully feel the water dripping down your body and appreciate the strength in your legs.
- **Mindful walking:** Concentrate on the connection between your foot and the earth with each step to cleanse your root chakra while giving your mind a break.
- **Pamper your feet:** Taking care of your feet is a way to care for your physical body and root chakra energy.
- **Meditate outdoors:** Meditating in nature and focusing on how your feet anchor you to the earth can make you feel safe and balanced in your body.
- **Use positive affirmations:** Saying positive affirmations, like "I am enough as I am," can help

you stay positive and remind you of your solid foundation.

- **Try a mudra:** Use the root chakra mudra by interlacing your fingers and extending your middle fingers to touch while keeping your thumbs and index fingers in a ring shape. Optionally, lower your arms and flip the mudra upside down to point the middle fingers at your pelvic region.

Sacral: Your Second Chakra

The sacral chakra, also known as the *Svadhisthana* chakra, is located below the navel, and is associated with the color orange. The sacral chakra's sign is an orange flower with six petals around its center. The cycles of birth, death, and rebirth are shown by the spirals on the lotus flower petals. Its element is water, and the recommended crystals include carnelian and moonstone. The water element is all about flow, flexibility, and freedom of expression when it comes to emotions and sensuality. Recommended yoga poses for the sacral chakra include pigeon pose and lizard pose. Blockage signs can include feelings of guilt, shame, and lack of creativity. The sacral chakra controls the reproductive organs and is associated with our sense of pleasure, emotions, creativity, and overall enjoyment of life. When this chakra is balanced and functioning properly, we can expect our relationship with ourselves and the world to feel harmonious, pleasureful, and nurturing.

When you work with this chakra, you'll think about how you relate to both other people and yourself. You'll find out that you have infinite creative power and learn how to have a fulfilling relationship. You'll also learn more about your fallback responses and innermost emotions and how to manage them. You will feel more comfortable telling people what you want, what you need, and how you feel. You'll learn how to say what's on your mind and how to start setting healthy boundaries.

Signs of a Blocked Sacral Chakra

When the sacral chakra is out of whack, you might feel any of the following:

- persistent pain in your lower back
- cysts on the ovaries
- fertility problems
- urinary tract infections (UTIs)
- pain during sexual activities
- problems with your kidneys and bladder
- other pelvic–lower abdominal issues

Blocked chakras can have a big effect on how we think and feel. Psychologically, blocked sacral energy can show up as problems like codependency or feeling like our emotions are taking over. Your sacral chakra may also be blocked if you have:

- too many sexual fantasies
- no desire for sex at all
- trouble expressing your feelings, needs, and creative ideas

How to Unblock Your Sacral Chakra

Even though certain habits and imbalances in the body, mind, and soul can block the chakras, with the right tools and care, we can re-align these energy centers. Here are some ways to:

- Focus on sacral area yoga poses, for example, goddess, happy baby, and Malasana poses.
- Use stones and crystals, such as carnelian or tiger's eye.

- Take a bath with essential oils to relax.
- Get in touch with your creative side by writing, dancing, making art, or doing whatever you like.
- Try saying positive things; examples provided at the link below:

https://www.throughthephases.com/powerful-sacral-chakra-affirmations/

When the sacral chakra is clear and balanced, you will have energy for creative thinking, movement, reproduction, desire, sexual fulfillment, and relationships. In relationships, you will be able to say what you want and need, and pleasure will be a priority.

Solar Plexus: Your Third Chakra

The solar plexus chakra (*Manipura*) is positioned above your navel, at the center of your torso, and is related to the color yellow. Its element is fire. Citrine and yellow calcite are good crystals to use with it. The boat pose and the plank are yoga poses to assist with clearing this chakra. Low self-esteem, self-doubt, and a lack of willpower can be signs of a blockage. The solar plexus chakra is in charge of the digestive system and is linked to our sense of self-worth, personal power, and confidence.

Signs of a Blocked Solar Plexus Chakra

Here are some signs of a blocked solar plexus chakra:

- low self-esteem and lack of confidence
- digestive problems like bloating, constipation, or diarrhea
- anxiety, stress, tension headaches, and muscle spasms
- control and trust issues
- lack of motivation and willpower to pursue your goals

- feeling stuck or stagnant in your life
- other physical symptoms like fatigue

How to Unblock the Solar Plexus Chakra
Here are some effective methods you can try:

- **Yoga:** Practicing yoga can help balance and open the solar plexus chakra. Poses that focus on the core, such as boat pose or warrior III, can be particularly beneficial.
- **Meditate:** Meditation is a powerful tool for balancing all the chakras, including the solar plexus. You can try visualization techniques that focus on the color yellow, or use affirmations related to personal power and confidence.
- **Practice deep breathing:** Breathing exercises can help release tension and stimulate the solar plexus chakra. For example, alternate nostril breathing or diaphragmatic breathing.
- **Use essential oils:** Oils like ginger, lemon, and peppermint can be used to stimulate and balance the solar plexus chakra. You can diffuse them, apply them topically, or add them to your bath.
- **Use crystals:** Crystals like citrine, yellow calcite, and tiger's eye are associated with the solar plexus chakra and can help balance its energy. You can carry them with you or place them on your abdomen during meditation.
- **Practice self-care:** Self-care like taking a relaxing bath, getting a massage, or spending time in nature can help balance the solar plexus chakra and reduce stress and anxiety.
- **Focus on your diet:** Eating foods that are fiber-rich and don't contain processed sugar can help support

your digestive system and balance your solar plexus chakra. You can also try incorporating yellow foods like peppers, bananas, and pineapples into your diet.

Heart: Your Fourth Chakra

Your heart chakra (*Anahata*) is positioned in the middle of your chest. Its color is green or pink and the associated crystals are rose quartz, green aventurine, emerald, or rhodonite. It's associated with the element of air. Recommended yoga: the camel, fish, and cobra pose.

It controls: Love, compassion, forgiveness, relationships, acceptance, inner peace, emotional healing, balance, harmony, and empathy. Balance, peace, and calmness are all things that are linked to the heart chakra as well. When you are worried or stressed, your brain takes over and blocks your feelings which then blocks your heart chakra. This makes you feel both mentally and physically off.

Signs of Heart Chakra Blockage:

- lack of love and compassion
- feelings of emptiness
- being shy and having social anxiety
- being too hard on yourself and other people
- feelings of resentment and anger
- not being able to give or take freely
- sense of insecurity and fear of intimacy in close relationships
- jealousy
- heart and lung problems

How to Unblock Your Heart Chakra

- **Surround yourself with green:** The heart chakra can be opened by wearing green clothes or jewelry and lighting green candles. It can also be opened and balanced with the help of chakra healing crystals, like emerald, malachite, jade, and green tourmaline.
- **Meditation and yoga:** Meditation and yoga can help heal the heart chakra when they are done regularly. Imagine a ball of green healing light in your chest and do deep breathing or pranayama exercises to stimulate the element of air associated with your Anahata.
- **Volunteer:** Giving back to others can help release fears and blockages. Choose a charity that resonates with you and allows you to share your talents with others. Being outdoors is even better for healing in the fresh air.
- **Let go of negative emotions:** Practice letting go of anger or fear in your everyday life. When negative emotions arise, take a deep breath, and imagine a green light washing it away, filling you with love. This will help you avoid negative patterns and react from a place of compassion.

Throat: Your Fifth Chakra

The throat chakra is positioned in the middle of the neck and is responsible for the passage of energy between the lower parts of the body and the head. The principle of expression and communication is at the heart of the throat chakra's work.

The most common Sanskrit name for the throat chakra is *Vishuddha*, which means "pure" or "purification." This chakra is related to the element of sound and is an important instrument of communication and expression.

The throat chakra is represented with the color blue

turquoise or aquamarine blue, and the auric color can also be seen as smoky purple or turquoise.

The symbol for the throat chakra is a circle with 16 petals and a crescent with a circle within it. Very often, it's signified by a circle involving a downward-pointing triangle in which another circle is embedded. The petals are a smoky purple or grayish lavender color.

The throat chakra is typically located at the level of the throat, but it has a multidimensional aspect that extends out of the front of the throat and in the back at a slight upward angle. It is connected to various parts of the body, including the mouth, jaws, tongue, pharynx, palate, shoulders, and neck. The gland associated with this chakra is the thyroid, which plays a vital role in regulating the body's energy processing through temperature, growth, and metabolism.

The throat chakra is also associated with certain psychological and behavioral characteristics, such as the ability to express oneself truthfully and communicate effectively, both verbally and non-verbally. It is also linked to the more subtle realms of spirit and intuitive abilities, as well as the ability to project ideas and blueprints into reality and realize one's purpose and vocation. Additionally, it is associated with a good sense of timing.

Opening the throat chakra can help align one's vision with reality, release pressure on the heart chakra located below, and connect to the etheric body, which holds the blueprint or perfect template of the other dimensions of the body. The throat chakra also has a natural connection to the sacral chakra, which is the center of emotions and creativity.

Signs of a Blocked Throat Chakra

Your throat chakra can become blocked or imbalanced, which can affect one's overall wellbeing. Signs of a blocked throat chakra may include:

- difficulty expressing oneself
- feeling shy or insecure
- inability to speak up for yourself or others
- fear of speaking in public
- consistently lying or being deceitful
- difficulty being a good listener
- struggling with communication in relationships
- voice problems or frequent sore throats
- trouble being creative
- feeling stuck or uninspired in life

These signs can indicate a need to work on balancing the throat chakra to improve communication, expression, creativity, and overall wellbeing.

How to Unblock Your Throat Chakra

There are several ways to balance the throat chakra:

- **Express yourself:** Speak your truth, even if it's uncomfortable. Write down your thoughts and feelings in a journal.
- **Engage in creative activities:** Do something creative that you enjoy, like painting, singing, or dancing.
- **Practice yoga:** Certain yoga poses, like the Plow Pose or the Fish Pose, can help open the throat chakra.
- **Meditate:** Sit quietly and focus on your breath. Visualize a blue light surrounding your throat area and allowing it to open and release any blockages.
- **Use healing crystals:** Blue crystals, like aquamarine, lapis lazuli, or blue apatite, can be placed on the throat or worn as jewelry.
- **Use essential oils:** Essential oils, like peppermint, lavender, or chamomile, can be diffused or applied topically to help balance the throat chakra.

- **Engage in communication:** Practice active listening and effective communication with others. Speak clearly and kindly.
- **Spend time in nature:** Spend time outdoors in natural surroundings, like a park or a garden, to help calm the mind and connect with your inner self.

Third Eye: Your Sixth Chakra

The third eye chakra, also known as the *Ajna* chakra, is located at the center of the forehead, between the eyebrows. The color associated with this chakra is indigo, a deep blue-purple shade. The third eye chakra is associated with the element of light and the sense of intuition.

There are several crystals that are believed to be helpful in balancing and activating the third eye chakra, including amethyst, lapis lazuli, and clear quartz. These crystals are thought to amplify intuition, enhance mental clarity, and increase awareness of one's own spiritual path.

Yoga poses that are recommended for balancing the third eye chakra include child's pose, eagle pose, and seated, forward fold. These poses help to bring focus and concentration to the forehead area and enhance overall awareness.

The third eye chakra is associated with the pituitary gland and governs the body's pineal gland, eyes, and the brain's left and right hemispheres. When balanced, it promotes intuition, psychic abilities, imagination, and creativity. It also assists in accessing higher states of consciousness, connecting with one's inner wisdom and spiritual growth.

Signs That the Third Eye Chakra Is Blocked

When the third eye chakra is blocked, it can manifest as feelings of confusion, lack of direction, or inability to make decisions. Physical symptoms may include headaches, eye problems, and sinus issues. One may feel disconnected from their intuition and find it difficult to trust their own inner guidance.

How to Unblock the Third Eye Chakra

To unblock the third eye chakra, there are several practices that one can incorporate into their daily routine. Meditation is particularly useful for activating this chakra, as it promotes relaxation and inner peace. Journaling and other creative pursuits can also help to stimulate intuition and imagination. Practicing yoga poses that focus on the third eye chakra can also be beneficial. Spending time in nature, particularly around water, can also help to clear and balance this chakra. Finally, practicing gratitude and positive affirmations can help to shift one's mindset and promote feelings of inner peace and clarity.

Crown: Your Seventh Chakra

The crown chakra is positioned at the top of the head. Its color is violet or white, and it is associated with the element of consciousness or pure awareness. Some crystals that can be used to balance the crown chakra include amethyst, clear quartz, and selenite.

Yoga poses that are recommended for the crown chakra include headstand, tree pose, and lotus pose. These poses help to stimulate the crown chakra and promote the flow of energy through the body.

The crown chakra is associated with the highest level of consciousness and represents our connection to the divine. It controls the upper brain and the nervous system, and it is responsible for spiritual awakening, enlightenment, and self-realization.

Signs of a Blocked Crown Chakra

- feeling disconnected from spirituality
- a lack of purpose or direction in life
- confusion and a disconnection from one's body

- physical symptoms such as headaches, migraines, or dizziness

How to Unblock the Crown Chakra

To unblock the crown chakra, one can engage in meditation, prayer, or other spiritual practices. Practicing gratitude, connecting with nature, and spending time in quiet contemplation can also help to open the crown chakra. Using affirmations, practicing forgiveness, and seeking guidance from a spiritual teacher or mentor can help to release any blockages and promote a sense of connection to the divine.

YOUR CHANCE TO HELP ANOTHER INNER CHILD

Perhaps you've begun the HEAL process by now, or maybe you're ready to get started... Either way, you're in the perfect position to share it with someone else so they too can reach peace and healing.

Simply by sharing your honest opinion of this book on Amazon, you'll show new readers where they can find all the information they need to heal their inner child.

LET'S HEAR FROM YOU!
IF YOU ENJOYED THIS BOOK, PLEASE LEAVE A REVIEW TO HELP OTHERS

Thank you so much for your support. In every adult, there's a child – and every child deserves to be taken care of.

Scan the QR code to leave your review!

https://geni.us/LyGmoq

CONCLUSION

It takes courage to grow up and become who you really are. –E.E. Cummings

I wrote *Inner Child Healing* to delve into the complicated nature of the inner child and how to heal it. As someone who has gone through this journey myself, I know firsthand the pain and struggle that comes with having a wounded inner child. Through my own experiences and research, I have come to understand the importance of healing the inner child and how it can positively impact our lives.

Throughout the book, I shared information and tools to help readers heal their inner child. One of the key takeaways is understanding where the inner child came from and how classical conditioning and familial trauma affected it. It's crucial to listen to the inner child's internal conversation and learn how to discern the beliefs, thoughts, feelings, and automatic responses that arise from this.

Additionally, the book highlights typical signs of an inner child who has been hurt, the HEAL journey, and steps to take to prepare for it. We also discussed how to use the twin flame journey to practice self-love and make the inner child whole. Setting boundaries to protect and heal the inner child is essential, and we also explored chakra healing for each of the seven parts of the inner child.

But healing the inner child is not just about the steps and tools; it's about the journey and the transformation that takes place within us. As I mentioned previously, I used inner child work to heal myself and manage my inner child through the step-by-step process. And now, I'd like to encourage others to do the same.

To those who have tried the HEAL process, I invite and encourage you to share your success stories. It's essential to celebrate our progress and inspire others who may be going through a similar journey.

I wish all readers the best on their journey to inner child healing. It takes courage, patience, and persistence, but I know that you have what it takes to be successful and let your light shine bright enough for others. Embrace the part of the child inside you that smiles and spreads joy. Be authentic and happy with who you are and let that radiate outwards.

Overall, *Inner Child Healing* is an enlightening book that gives readers the tools they need to heal their inner child and live better, more fulfilling lives. If you've enjoyed reading this book, I would greatly appreciate it if you could rate it and share your experience with me. Together, we can continue to spread the message of inner child healing and create a world where everyone can heal and thrive.

AUTHOR BIO

S. M. Weng, the author of *Inner Child Healing,* faced many challenges in her younger life. When she was merely four years old, her parents got angry with her and told her that she was behaving badly. Many years later she could recognize that her behavior was normal in relation to what most kids at that age do. In this booked filled with valuable tips for the readers, Susye explains:

"What really hurt me the most is that they told me that they would throw me away. It made me feel worthless and scared."

How many of us have experienced similar feelings of rejection, hurt, abandonment, and fear in our younger years?

When Susye saw these kinds of issues being mentioned repeatedly among her social media followers, she could relate and decided to embark on the journey of writing this book.

"As a four-year-old girl, I panicked; and unknowingly, I never recovered from this event. It was only much later in life, as an adult, when I went into inner child meditation to unblock my fear of abandonment, that I made peace with that experience."

Susye shares her knowledge on why we respond and behave the way we do and why we believe lies about our worth.

She traveled the world and used her experiences as opportunities to find answers in ancient practices.

After trying and testing many methods, she used what she had learned from psychology and spiritualism to perfect her approach. In *Inner Child Healing*, she talks about combining Western and Eastern culture in a unique "HEAL" process with practical tips you can follow daily, and she uniquely focuses on inner child meditation to complete the integration and healing process.

REFERENCES

Aguirre, R. T., & Galen, G. W. (2017). Self-image and narcissism in college students. *Journal of College Student Psychotherapy*, 31(1), 1-13.

Alan Keith Tillotson, Nai-Shing Hu Tillotson, & Abel, R. (2001). *The one Earth herbal sourcebook : everything you need to know about Chinese, Western, and Ayurvedic herbal treatments*. Twin Streams.

Amaral, R. (2018, November 2). *How beliefs affect thoughts and behaviours*. Psychology for Growth. https://psychologyforgrowth.com/2018/11/02/how-beliefs-affect-thoughts-and-behaviours/

American Psychological Association. (2018). *Stress Effects on the Body*. American Psychological Association. https://www.apa.org/topics/stress/body

Andrade, S. (2021, July 1). *Council Post: The Importance Of Setting Healthy Boundaries*. Forbes. https://www.forbes.com/sites/forbescoachescouncil/2021/07/01/the-importance-of-setting-healthy-boundaries/?sh=3d380c5e56e4

Baumeister, R. F. (1999). *The self in social psychology*. Psychology Press.

Bee, H. (1992). *The developing child*. Harper Collins.

Cameron, Y. (2009, October 28). *A Beginner's Guide To The 7 Chakras*. Mind Body Green. https://www.mindbodygreen.com/articles/7-chakras-for-beginners

Campbell, L. (2016, May 17). *Personal Boundaries: Types and How to Set Them*. Psych Central. https://www.psychcentral.com/lib/what-are-personal-boundaries-how-do-i-get-some#how-to-set-boundaries

Carl Ransom Rogers. (1959). *A Theory of Therapy, Personality, and Interpersonal Relationships: Vol. Vol. 3: Formulations of the person and the social context*. (In (ed.) S. Koch, Psychology: A study of science.). McGraw Hill.

Cassata, C. (2019, September 3). *Why You Don't Need a Lot of Time or Money to Make Self-Care a Priority*. Healthline Media. https://www.healthline.com/health-news/self-care-is-not-just-treating-yourself

Chalfant, M. (2018, March 21). *A Guided-Meditation for Setting Goals and Achieving Success*. On YouTube. https://www.youtube.com/watch?v=3lRWSACf5vY

Cherry, K. (2022, September 7). *What You Should Know About the Peripheral Nervous System*. Verywell Mind. https://www.verywellmind.com/what-is-the-peripheral-nervous-system-2795465

Cherry, K. (2023a, February 23). *How Classical Conditioning works: an Overview with Examples*. Verywell Mind. https://www.verywellmind.com/classical-conditioning-2794859

Cherry, K. (2023b, March 13). *Child Development Theories and Examples*. Verywell Mind. https://www.verywellmind.com/child-development-theories-2795068

CPTSD Foundation. (2020, July 13). *The Wounded Inner Child*. CPTSD Foundation. https://cptsdfoundation.org/2020/07/13/the-wounded-inner-child/

Cikanavičius, D. (2018, May 14). *5 Ways Childhood Neglect and Trauma Skews Our Self-Esteem*. Psych Central. https://psychcentral.com/blog/psychology-self/2018/05/childhood-self-esteem

Dalien, S. (2015, January 22). *Children Learn Through Their Environment | SpecialEdResource.com*. Special Ed Resource. https://specialedresource.com/children-learn-through-their-environment

EOC Institute. (n.d.). *Chart: How Meditation Unleashes Subconscious Mind Power*. EOC Institute. Retrieved April 24, 2023, from https://eocinstitute.org/meditation/how-to-harness-your-subconscious-mind-

Encyclopaedia of Early Childhood Development. (2023, January). *Social violence | Effects of Physical Family and Community Violence on Child Development*. Encyclopedia on Early Childhood Development. https://www.child-encyclopedia.com/social-violence/according-experts/effects-physical-family-and-community-violence-child-development

Exploring Your Mind. (2017, December 9). *From the Subconscious Mind to the Conscious Mind*. Exploring Your Mind. https://exploringyourmind.com/subconscious-mind-conscious-mind/

Gillespie, C. (2020, October 27). *Generational Trauma Might Explain Your Anxiety and Depression—Here's What It Means*. Health. https://www.health.com/condition/ptsd/generational-trauma

Gartner, J. (2016). Understanding and treating self-erasure. *Journal of Clinical Psychology*, 72(10), 1012-1022.

Great Meditation. (2021, December 8). *Guided Meditation For Inner Child Healing*. Www.youtube.com. https://www.youtube.com/watch?v=olmV_appq9I

Great Meditation. (2022). Inner Child Healing | 10 Minute Guided Meditation. On YouTube. https://www.youtube.com/watch?v=HCZXr4UNCk8

Heyl, J. (2023, February 14). *What Are the 7 Chakras and What Do They Mean?* Verywell Mind. https://www.verywellmind.com/the-7-chakras-and-what-they-mean-7106518

Hoffman, J. (2018). Feeling not good enough: The silent epidemic. *The Journal of Individual Psychology*, 74(2), 80-89.

Holland, K. (2018, October 17). *Positive Self-Talk: How Talking to Yourself Is a*

Good Thing. Healthline; Healthline Media. https://www.healthline.-com/health/positive-self-talk#benefits-of-self--talk

Jacobson, S. (2017, March 23). *What is the "Inner Child"?* Harley Therapy Blog. https://www.harleytherapy.co.uk/counselling/what-is-the-inner-child.htm

Jenkins, S. (2009, August 26). *Money and the Inner Child.* GoodTherapy.org Therapy Blog. https://www.goodtherapy.org/blog/money-and-the-inner-child/

Lewis, M. (1990). *Self-knowledge and social development in early life.* New York: Guilford. (In L. A. Pervin (Ed.), Handbook of personality, pp. 277–300).

Lindberg, S. (2020, August 24). *What Are Chakras? Meaning, Location, and How to Unblock Them.* Healthline. https://www.healthline.com/health/what-are-chakras#about-chakras

Lumo Health. (n.d.). *How to heal your inner child.* My Therapy Assistant. https://www.mytherapyassistant.com/blog/do-you-have-a-wounded-inner-child-here-are-7-key-signs

Make One Smile. (n.d.). *500 Best Quotes about Life that will change you | Great Quotes about Life.* Make One Smile. Retrieved April 24, 2023, from https://makeonesmile.blogspot.com/2018/11/500-best-quotes-about-life-that-will-change-you-great-quotes-about-life.html

Mcleod, S. (2008). *Self-Concept | Simply Psychology.* Simplypsychology.org; Simply Psychology. https://www.simplypsychology.org/self-concept.html

Mcleod, S. (2022, November 3). *Self-Concept in Psychology: Definition, Development, Examples.* Simply Psychology. https://simplypsychology.org/self-concept.html

Mindworks Team. (2017, December 18). *What Is Self-Reflection Meditation? Benefits of Meditation Reflection.* Mindworks Meditation. https://mindworks.org/blog/self-reflection-meditation

Monroe, A. (n.d.). *Chakra Healing: 9 Amazing Ways To Clear Your Chakras.* Www.psychics4today.com. https://www.psychics4today.com/chakra-healing/

Miller, A. (2019). Self-love, self-care, and mental health. *Journal of the American Academy of Psychiatry and the Law,* 47(4), 498-502.

Parenting For Brain. (2019, July 25). *Classical vs Operant Conditioning.* Parenting-ForBrain. https://www.parentingforbrain.com/classical-vs-operant-conditioning/

Pikörn, I. (2019, August 30). *Noticing, Healing and Freeing Your Inner Child.* Insight Timer Blog. https://insighttimer.com/blog/inner-child-meaning-noticing-healing-freeing

Positive Creators. (2020, March 9). *How Does The Subconscious Mind Create Reality.* Positivecreators.com. https://positivecreators.com/how-does-the-subconscious-mind-create-reality/

Raypole, C. (2021, February 5). *Habit Loop: What It Is and How to Break It.* Healthline. https://www.healthline.com/health/mental-health/habit-loop

Scott, E. (2022, May 24). *The Toxic Effects of Negative Self-Talk.* Verywell Mind. https://www.verywellmind.com/negative-self-talk-and-how-it-affects-us-4161304

Shah, P. (2020, April 2). *What the Chakras Teach Us About the Mind and Body Connection.* Chopra. https://chopra.com/articles/what-the-chakras-teach-us-about-the-mind-and-body-connection

Shapiro, L. E. (2018). *Understanding and treating anxiety disorders: An integrative approach to healing the wounded self.* American Psychological Association.

Stokes, V. (2021, December 6). *Want to Deepen Your Sensuality? Look to the Sacral Chakra.* Healthline. https://www.healthline.com/health/mind-body/sacral-chakra

Thomas, D. (2023, January 30). *Highly Inspirational David Goggins Quotes.* Your Positive Oasis. https://yourpositiveoasis.com/david-goggins-quotes/

Thomas, G. O., Poortinga, W., & Sautkina, E. (2016). Habit Discontinuity, Self-Activation, and the Diminishing Influence of Context Change: Evidence from the UK Understanding Society Survey. *PLOS ONE, 11*(4), e0153490. https://doi.org/10.1371/journal.pone.0153490

University of Minnesota. (n.d.). *Reflective Practices.* Bakken Center for Spirituality & Healing. https://csh.umn.edu/academics/whole-systems-healing/reflective-practices

Wible, P. (2021, April 13). *Did your wounded child choose your career?* Pamela Wible MD. https://www.idealmedicalcare.org/did-your-wounded-child-choose-your-career/

Wisneski, L., & Anderson, L. (2005). The Scientific Basis of Integrative Medicine. *Evidence-Based Complementary and Alternative Medicine, 2*(2), 257–259. https://doi.org/10.1093/ecam/neh079

York Morris, S. (2016, July 12). *What Are the Benefits of Self-Talk?* Healthline; Healthline Media. https://www.healthline.com/health/mental-health/self-talk

Zander, M. (2019). *The Age of Reason.* Scholastic.com. https://www.scholastic.com/parents/family-life/social-emotional-learning/development-milestones/age-reason.html

ALSO BY S. M. WENG

INNER CHILD *Healing*

Discover Your True Self, Overcome Childhood Trauma, and Deepen Relationships With Self-Love, Chakra Healing, and Twin Flame Connection

S. M. Weng

INNER CHILD *Healing*

COLORING BOOK

S. M. Weng

INNER CHILD *Healing*

JOURNALING PROMPTS

S. M. Weng

SANA A TU *Niño Interior*

Descubre a tu verdadero yo, supera los traumas de la infancia y profundiza tus vínculos con amor propio, la sanación de chakras y la conexión con tu llama gemela

S. M. Weng

EMPATH
— AND —
PSYCHIC
POWERS AWAKENED

Ignite Your Inner Potential and Manifest Spiritual
Fulfillment by **Embracing Self-Love, Divine Healing,** and
the **Effortless Flow of the Twin Flame Connection.**

S. M. WENG

SELF-LOVE
for
WOMEN
on the
TWIN FLAME JOURNEY

7 SIGNS YOU'RE ON THE RIGHT PATH,
NAVIGATE SHADOW WORK, CONQUER LOVE'S OBSTACLES,
AND NURTURE POSITIVE SELF-TALK FOR 11:11 UNION

S. M. WENG

Printed in Great Britain
by Amazon